Praise for *Story*

"A journey full of wonder, tears, joy, despair, and hope revealed through the eyes and heart of a storyteller."

—*Publishers Weekly*, starred review

"It is a potpourri of language and imagery, mingled to delicious effect, calling the reader to see the gospel story with fresh eyes, breaking through the numbness of familiarity to expose the wonder and adventure God offers. This highly original retelling of the Scripture is often beautiful, often haunting, and thoroughly compelling. It is a reminder that Christ's promise of 'life, anew' is constantly with us, then, now, and always."

—*BookPage*

"I loved it so much that I am going right out to buy it so that I can loan it out to people. Beautiful poetry. The story I have always known and wanted to tell, told as I have imagined telling it. Using stories, poetry, memories, scriptures, and a childlike wonderment that is disarming and playful. I wish I had written it. Simply fantastic."

—garagebandtheatre.blogspot.com

"Storyteller Steven James assumes an enormous responsibility in this slim volume: retelling the entire story of redemption for a postmodern audience that needs to hear—and experience—that story in a fresh and powerful way. In the hands of a lesser writer, such a task could easily fall flat. Not so with James . . . Everything in this book—every image, every metaphor, every thought, every sentence—points the way to the cross and the resurrection and the profound love of God. *Story* resonates with both the postmodern seeker and the mature Christian who longs for a fresh experience with God."

—FaithfulReader.com

"James's luxuriant writing is deeply perceptive of the divinity, humanity, and mystery of Christ. The book is an astonishingly personal journey of God's love for weak, fallen humanity. Comparing the Bible story to a true fairy tale, we're called to awaken with Christ."

—*CBA Retailers + Resources*

"The greatest story ever told—that of Jesus—is retold in this book, *Story*, by one of America's most brilliant young authors, Steven James. His poetry, written in short lines with no caps, is lyrical and powerful—beautiful and often painful to read. If you want a book to make you view Jesus and the story of the Bible from a whole different vantage point, to feel his pain and wonder of it again, this is that book to savor and treasure."

—ChristianBookPreviews.com

"The greatest story ever told is recapped in short excerpts, building verse-by-verse in a modern fashion, as the reader journeys through this cleverly crafted book. From the manger to the cross, James connects the dots and uses modern-day examples to create a trendy devotional-like book that is an easy yet enjoyable read."

—*CCM Magazine*

"James has a gift of relating the story of the Bible to life today. In this incredible book, professional storyteller Steven James tackles the greatest story of them all: the story of redemption. James's grasp of language is breathtaking and his power of description unequaled."

—National Women's Ministries Department of the Assemblies of God

"*Story* is a book that will give you a new perspective on the intricately woven tales the Bible offers. Both deep enough for longtime believers and simple enough for the curious, Steven James has done a good job making this information interesting, humorous, understandable, and relevant."

—1340mag.com

"*Story* retells the Christian story in a way that is fresh and brings new life. After hearing the Easter story in drab ways for years, it can lose its punch. Use *Story* to breathe new life into the story of Christ's death and resurrection."

—*Relevant Media Group*

STORY

Our Journey of
Heartache and Grace from
Eden to Evermore

STEVEN JAMES

Revell
a division of Baker Publishing Group
Grand Rapids, Michigan

Published by Revell
a division of Baker Publishing Group
P.O. Box 6287, Grand Rapids, MI 49516-6287
www.revellbooks.com

New paperback edition published 2012
ISBN 978-0-8007-2065-0

Printed in the United States of America

The Library of Congress has cataloged the original edition as follows:
James, Steven, 1969-
    Story : recapture the mystery / Steven James.
        p.   cm.
    ISBN 10: 0-8007-3113-1 (pbk.)
    ISBN 978-0-8007-3113-7 (pbk.)
    1. Bible stories, English. I. Title.
BS551.3.J36 2006
220.9'505—dc22   2005022984

12   13   14   15   16   17   18   7   6   5   4   3   2   1

for Pamela

table of contents

acknowledgments

Special thanks to the monks at the Abbey of Gethsemani in rural Kentucky for providing a place where the seeds of this book could begin poking through the soil, to Esther, Kristin, Liesl, Roger, and Todd for your insights and suggestions, and to the kind folks at Baker Publishing Group for giving this book a chance. Thanks.

introduction

When I was in ninth grade, my church's youth group performed an Easter play. Actually, it was a pre-Easter play because it was only about the betrayal and death of Jesus, not his rising. We performed it on the Friday before Easter. "It's called a Tenebrae service," said our pastor. "It means *service of darkness.*"

I got to play Jesus, probably because I had the longest hair of any of the guys in my class.

Since I was Jesus I had quite a few lines, but the only one I still remember is this: "My God, my God, why hast Thou forsaken me?" I actually had to say, "Why hast Thou forsaken me?" because our denomination still used the 380-year-old King James translation of the Bible.

Our church was over one hundred years old and had rows of looming stained glass windows rising to the ceiling. During our evening rehearsals they looked like black towers lining the walls. It was cold that spring; the radiators in the church weren't strong enough to chase away the chill in the air.

At our last dress rehearsal, I stepped onstage barefoot and wearing my bedsheet. Jesus didn't actually die wearing a bedsheet; I'm pretty sure he was naked at the time. But if our church wasn't even ready for a twentieth-century translation of the Bible, we certainly weren't ready for a naked ninth grader with skinny legs standing next to the pulpit yelling, "Why hast Thou forsaken me?"

I cleared my throat and called out to the empty, chilly sanctuary, "My God, my God, why hast Thou forsaken me?" My words bounced off the black windows.

My voice was changing at the time, and I probably sounded more like a five-year-old girl at a tea party than a thirty-three-year-old convicted criminal being tortured to death.

The pastor cringed. "Try it again."

"My God, my God, why hast Thou forsaken me?" I said as deeply as I could, sounding more like Batman this time than a little girl.

"We've been through this before, Steve. Say it like you mean it."

"I am."

"No, you're not."

"Yes, I am." I didn't really think he should be arguing with Jesus like that. Judas coughed. The girl playing Mary rolled her eyes at me. I think she was supposed to be my mother, but it was hard to tell. There were a bunch of Marys in the play.

"You've been abandoned by God," said my pastor, pacing in front of the pews. "You're about to die. You've been deserted by all your friends. You're alone on the cross suffering a horrible death. Say it like that. Like you mean it."

"Okay."

"All right."

"Yeah."

"Go ahead."

"Right." I paused for a moment. "Um, do I really have to say 'why hast Thou forsaken me?' It sounds kinda old-fashioned."

He took a long, slow breath and said, "Yes."

I sighed. "Okay, okay . . ." I cleared my throat. "Ahem. My God, my God, why hast Thou forsaken me?"

My pastor shook his head and rubbed his temples. I told him I was doing the best I could and that's all I could do anyhow and I can't help it if I'm not the best actor in the world and if he wanted someone who was perfect he should have chosen someone else to play the part. I had no idea at the time how true that statement was.

All the other kids were waiting for me to just get it right so we could get on with rehearsal and get it all over with. Judas had lost interest in what was happening onstage and was busy flirting with Mary, who was pretending to be *totally* annoyed by him like ninth-grade girls do when they really like someone. I'd heard they were going out, which was too bad for me since I kind of liked her. For a minute I forgot all about being rejected by God and thought about being rejected by Mary. *Man, she's cute. I'd love to go out with her—wait a minute, no, she's my mother.*

I was beginning to get very confused right about then.

The pastor looked at his watch. "Let's try it again."

"My God, my God, why hast Thou forsaken me?" I called again.

I never did get that line right.

Honestly, I don't even remember saying the line in the service. I guess I've blocked that out of my memory. I remember the darkness, though, swelling around us as the other kids from my class snuffed out one candle after the other. A deep, hungry darkness filled the church as the parishioners left in silence and I went back downstairs to change into my blue jeans and go home to play video games.

And I remember that day in rehearsal, standing in front of the empty church dressed in athletic shorts and a bedsheet, talking like Shakespeare, fantasizing about Mary while my pastor tried to get me to realize how the words must have sounded the first time they were said—coming from the throat of Jesus.

⸙

A few years ago, I walked into the living room just as the movie my wife was watching ended. She was sitting on the couch crying.

"Are you okay?" I asked.

She nodded.

"Is something wrong?"

She shook her head.

"Then why are you crying?"

She shrugged. Then she looked up at me sweetly and said, "I love you." I didn't have the slightest idea what was going on. They never prepare you for moments like these in premarital counseling.

"Okay," I said, somewhat suspiciously. "I love you too?" That had to be the right answer. When you're married, that's always the right answer.

Then she patted the couch next to her as the credits began to scroll up the TV screen, and I sat down. She snuggled close, dabbing at her eyes. "I guess you had to see the whole thing."

I put my arm around her. "Yeah, I guess so," I mumbled, but of course I didn't really think I would have cried. Not during a chick flick. And even if I did, I wouldn't have let her see me. Guys have to be careful about things like that.

Either way, when you miss most of the story and only walk in for the finale, you're not usually moved to tears.

⸙

During my last year of college I worked as a wilderness guide for a state correctional program for at-risk youth. We worked for six weeks and then had three weeks off. One of our trips coincided with Easter. I was in charge of logistics that week, and since the rest of the team was hiking nearby, I asked my boss for Easter Sunday off so I could go to church.

"Oh, are you a Christian?"

"Yeah, of course."

"Well, why don't you come with us—with my wife and I?"

I shrugged. "Sure. Okay. Why not."

As you remember, the church I'd grown up attending was really old and traditional. It had lots of organ music, candles, chanting, stained glass windows, and Jesus in a bedsheet. At my boss's church the closest things to stained glass windows were the tattoos on the arms of the greeters. There wasn't any organ, just an electric guitar and a drum set that took up half the stage. And the people didn't chant. They rocked out. They even brought their own tambourines. And they danced. People at my church never danced. At his church, the service felt like a wedding celebration. At mine, it sort of had the feel of a funeral. His church didn't even have a building; they just rented a room on the campus of Southern Illinois University.

The sermon wasn't all that memorable, but the joy of the people was. And that day something happened to me. Jesus didn't show up in a bedsheet. Somewhere between the dancing and the testimonies, he showed up in my heart.

I'd been telling people my whole life I was a Christian. I'd gone to church every Sunday as long as I could remember. I knew the story, or I thought I did. But I'd never been moved to tears. But that day, at last, it all started to make sense. For the first time, I began to see the sweep of the story, not just isolated scenes here or there. The whole story finally clicked together. *Oh, so that's what it means.*

I wouldn't say I didn't believe in God before that day; I think on some level I did. I'd accepted his reality but had never really embraced his presence. I knew about him, but at my boss's charismatic church on the Easter Sunday of my twenty-first year, I began to fall in love with God.

I understood.

I believed.

I finally realized what those words "My God, my God, why hast Thou forsaken me?" must have really sounded like back when Jesus died. Those words were spoken from the center of the greatest darkness of all—the darkness of a soul abandoned by God. I'd been aching my whole life to believe in something that ultimately mattered. That day, I didn't ache anymore.

I think I might have even cried. Just a little bit. But don't tell my wife.

Easter was a love story after all. I'd never seen that before.

And I was there, in the arms of God, in the final scene.

⅞·

For some people the true meaning of Easter gets lost somewhere in the labyrinth of religious tradition. That's the way it was for me. I knew the right words to say, the right time to stand up and sit down during the service, the proper way to act when a full platter of money was passed in front of you, but God didn't seem to have anything to do with the rest of my life. I would just come home each week and set my religion on a shelf again until the next service. A couple years ago I wrote a poem about it.

boxing god

come here, god, i'd like to keep you in this little shoe box. i'd like
to pull you out whenever i need you and put you away whenever i
don't. come on. climb in.

there you go . . . now, let me just slide this lid over the top and . . .
okay, now, i'll just set you here in the closet and keep you handy for
a rainy day . . .

hmm . . . i have to say, i didn't think you'd fit so easily. i actually
thought i might have to really pound on you to squeeze you in
there.

imagine that. pounding on you to make you fit! ha. how funny is
that?

well, g-bye. you be a good little god, now. don't go climbing out of
your box. i'll be back to feed you later.

That day at my boss's church, Jesus showed me that I was the one
boxed in. And he was the one lifting the lid to finally set me free.

For other people, the story of Easter has gotten overshadowed in the
secularism of political correctness gone amuck. We're not supposed to
wish people "Merry Christmas!" anymore, even though Christmas is a
nationally recognized holiday. I suppose Jesus doesn't belong in Easter
either. We can celebrate the spring equinox together, maybe. That should
be okay, but Jesus rising from the dead is taking things too far.

The bunny has upstaged the rabbi and stolen the show. The search
for plastic eggs has replaced the search for a missing body. Easter has
evolved into just another nice, harmless, spineless, little holiday with
the climax being a bunch of snot-nosed kids fighting over a piece of
chocolate, when it's supposed to be about a wrestling match between
life and death, a cosmic struggle between good and evil.

Easter has lots of lilies and spring hats and piles of fake, green, curly plastic grass stuff, but none of that has anything to do with the raw reality of a bloody cross and the final hope of the empty tomb.

The truth is, most people just aren't moved by the Easter story anymore. It's like we've walked in at the end of the movie and we just don't get what all the fuss is about.

"Is something wrong?"

The people who are crying shake their heads.

"Then why are you crying?"

To understand Easter, to really get it, I think you need to experience the whole story—enter the darkened theater, take your seat, and watch the tale unfold. Because the empty tomb doesn't make sense without the cross, the cross doesn't make sense without the manger in Bethlehem, and the manger doesn't make sense without the Garden of Eden.

It's all one story. And only when you finally untangle it, see its scope, and enter it for yourself do you realize that the story has finally entered and at last untangled you.

creation

i told my friend, "only children get excited over watching a butterfly."
but then he turned to me and said,
"so does
God."

> In the beginning God created the heavens and the earth. The earth
> was empty, a formless mass cloaked in darkness. And the Spirit of
> God was hovering over its surface. Then God said, "Let there be
> light," and there was light. And God saw that it was good.
>
> —*the opening words of the Bible (Genesis 1:1–4)*

Darkness and God lived side by side.

The Bible doesn't say anything about God creating the darkness. It was just "Let there be light"—no "Let there be dark." Apparently, darkness was already there before he ever spoke, just hanging around with God from the beginning of the beginning, from the edges of forever.

But I guess God finally got tired of the cloak of darkness, so he told his first story. He spoke and light appeared.

"Let there be," he said. And there was.

I'm not exactly sure why he did it. I don't think anyone knows his precise motivation. Personally, I think he got sick of the darkness. I think since God is love, he couldn't stand the thought of spending eternity alone in the dark without someone to love. He needed companionship because love gives, shares, sacrifices, woos. It has to. Or else it isn't love.

Ephesians 1:4–5 says, "Long ago, even before he made the world, God loved us and chose us in Christ to be holy and without fault in his eyes. His unchanging plan has always been to adopt us into his own family by bringing us to himself through Jesus Christ. And this gave him great pleasure." Those words really connect with me because if this universe was all part of God's adoption plans, then the origin of life on earth wasn't the product of chance or even intelligent design; it was all because of love.

According to that verse, before God created anything, he was daydreaming about me. At the dawn of time, I was on his mind. And so were you. While darkness swirled around him, he dreamt about us and he loved us. His unchanging plan has always been to have a close relationship with us. That was God's first dream, and it gave him great pleasure.

Then he shaped the world backward through time so that we would arrive at just the right moment in just the right place on just the right planet as part of a divine, intergalactic dream-come-true.

He couldn't adopt us into his family until he'd created a place for us to live, so he created the heavens and the earth. God spoke the first words and the darkness split in half. Light entered the universe. And God saw that it was good, so he kept going. He whispered out a full moon and shouted a billion stars into space so his children wouldn't have to look up at a lonely sky on that first night of their lives.

I'll leave the theological and cosmological and philosophical explanations of how he did it, and when he did it, and how long it actually took him to do it to the people who have the time and energy to study that sort of thing. I don't think it's really an integral part of the story. If it was, God would have been more careful to get us the specifics, maybe by handing Adam and Eve a doctoral dissertation explaining everything.

"Here, guys, this should clear it up. I cover the Big Bang theory, the fossil record, Neanderthals, carbon dating, and everything. And just so there's no confusion, I've included a timetable for you. The footnotes refer to a few websites that won't be written for a few millennia, so you can just skip those for now."

The point is, the Creator created. He did it. He spoke it. He hung the canvas of the universe with his words. He invented time and space in a single breath. God spoke, and comets and glaciers and stardust and volcanoes and gophers and platypuses became reality.

He formed mountains on the tip of his tongue, blew kisses of red dwarves into the far reaches of space, said the word and trees and flowers and animals blossomed and bloomed and bolted across the land. The sunrise of Easter had its origin at the dawn of time when darkness fled before the words of God.

> you clothe yourself with daylight.
> you wrap the stars around your waist.
> crickets chirp from the folds of your garments.
> grizzlies growl from the deep hidden pockets of your evening robe.
> where do you set me upon yourself?
> > am i an earring, dangling in the moonlight?
> > am i a necklace, flashing by your breast?
> where do you slip me on?
> where do i fit into your tale?
>
> and how do you wear so many of us
> at once?

Then God touched the earth and formed a man and a woman in his own image. It wasn't a physical likeness—how could it be if male and female were both created in the likeness of God?

By the way, I don't think being made in the likeness of God has anything to do with having toenails or tonsils or nipples or blue eyes or curly hair. Instead it includes stuff like being passionate about peace and quick to laugh and full of wonder and imagination and love and longing and life. Then God poured a questioning spirit into his children, along with dreams and persistence and salty tears and a dash of joy.

> And the LORD God formed a man's body from the dust of the ground and breathed into it the breath of life. And the man became a living person.... And the LORD God said, "It is not good for the man to be alone. I will make a companion who will help him." ... Then the LORD God made a woman ... and brought her to Adam.
>
> Genesis 2:7, 18, 22

> So God created people in his own image;
> God patterned them after himself;
> male and female he created them.
>
> Genesis 1:27

I think it's pretty cool that God made people—both male and female—in his own image. That probably drives both the chauvinists and the feminists nuts. And I'm always glad to see that happen. By fighting each other, we diminish ourselves. The image of God is found in our unity *as well as* our uniqueness. There's a great equality here. A completion of each other. Our fullness reflects his fullness. Males being male and females being female reflect a clearer, sharper image of the Creator.

And then God rested from his work. He stepped back and looked at this world teeming with life and hope and possibility, budding and growing and glistening everywhere, and looking forward to the future.

"Yeah, this is good," said God. "If I do say so myself, this is *really* good."

☙

oh, in the beginning, when you were alone,
    did you dream of someone like me?
in the beginning, from soil and stone,
when you breathed out a world to be . . .
    did you dream a great dream,
    did it glisten and gleam,
    for all of the angels to see?
in the beginning, in the depths of your heart,
were you thinking, already,
    of me?

significance.

harmony

the harpist plays strings fashioned by human hands,
and makes heavenly music.

what melodies you must make
strumming the strings you fashioned and strung
so deeply in my soul!

⸙

Now, although Adam and his wife were both naked, neither of them
felt any shame.

—*Moses, explaining the original innocence of humanity (Genesis 2:25)*

You should have seen Erik and Jamal play basketball together. They were on my high school hoops team, and both guys were All-Americans. It was pure poetry. Erik was our point guard, and Jamal was a six-foot-four forward with a thirty-six-inch vertical leap. Erik could weave a pass through a New York City rush hour, and Jamal knew how to defy gravity. They went together like popcorn and butter, like chips and salsa, like pizza and cold beer. In one game alone, Jamal had five consecutive dunks, two from Erik's alley-oops.

Once in a while you see an artist or an athlete or a musician step out of himself and disappear into his art and you sit there thinking, *He was made for this. He was* made *for this.* For Erik and Jamal, that happened on the basketball court. Pure poetry.

Throughout our lives we see moments of harmony, precision, symmetry, unbridled beauty, poetry in motion. But here's what I've been wondering lately: *why is it so rare?* You'd think in a world of seven billion people all striving to become more happy, successful, and fulfilled, we wouldn't have to look so hard to find those moments when life really rocks, when true harmony appears.

⚕

In the beginning, Adam and Eve lived without tension or regret. They had no prejudice, stress, hatred, rebellion, guilt, worry, or fear. They weren't ashamed of themselves or their choices or their God. Nothing had shattered the harmony. Nothing had splintered the original song. I can hardly imagine what that kind of world would be like.

We still see glimpses of the good, fragments of beauty, echoes of the holy, but it's always marred on this planet of unwanted pregnancies, school shootings, white lies, brain tumors, junk mail, terrorist attacks, political spin, sprained ankles, corporate cover-ups, AIDS, gossip, indigestion, heartache, and big angry dogs. We know harmony is possible, but it's so elusive. Most of us spend our entire lives trying to recapture it, to hear it clearly once again. And most of us fail.

And shame? Well, we don't like to think about that too much. We ignore our failures and downplay our moral meltdowns, and we fill our lives with frantic distractions so we can avoid noticing the splinter of guilt embedded so deeply in our souls.

But it was different in Eden. Adam and Eve spent time one-on-one with God, and nothing got in the way. No shame. No fear. No posturing. No religion. Just harmony, playing itself out in the synchronicity of creation.

Adam was one note, Eve another, and God a third. And they were woven together in a melody of relationship none of us has ever come close to recapturing. We hear faint echoes of that original song. But we haven't heard the whole thing. Not for a long, long time.

Once when I was in Los Angeles I saw a woman hailing a cab. And for just a moment, everything was perfect:

> her hair leaps out
> and curls and dances
> across her head in the puff of wind
> that seems to follow her everywhere
> and it freezes her hair for a moment in midair
> just like in those glossy pictures of
> beautiful women.
>
> and i wish that she would autograph
> the moment for me,
> but the breeze is gone before she can pick up a pen.
> and once again
> she looks normal
> and her hair looks
> very, very lonely.

No one's life is totally in tune anymore. During his sophomore year, Erik got a girl pregnant and was eventually kicked out of school. Jamal cheated on his algebra tests, lost his temper, and was accused of date raping someone in my class. Both managed to play a year or two of college ball before injuries or personal problems or whatever drove them from the court.

☙

Whenever I see a science fiction version of utopia in a novel or a movie, I'm always left wondering, *Is that the best we can do?* Sure, the people are well cared for. Sickness is gone. No one has dandruff or bad breath or zits. Little boys don't fight, argue, or miss the toilet. Little girls don't kick, scream, whine, or pout. Instead they just share the toys and giggle a lot and play nicely with their little brothers. Adults don't sweat, swear, conquer, compete, pass kidney stones, throw golf clubs, or get depressed. No one gets warts or stretch marks. Everything is provided. Everyone is happy . . . I guess.

Danger is gone. Temptation is gone. Life is safe and comfortable and secure and predictable. But of course there's no adventure anymore. No thrills, no risks, no new frontiers, no new challenges, just happiness—if you can call it that. If you call a life of no excitement, no struggle, no passion, and no uncertainty *happiness*. I can think of better words for it.

I think there's a reason bedtime stories always end with "happily ever after." Once everything is happy and there's no struggle, then there's no more story to tell. We don't want to hear about happiness and peace unless the story also includes freedom and discovery. Without discovery all you have is monotony. Without freedom, utopia isn't paradise after all. It's just hell in a fancy prom dress.

But God can create a better paradise than that. I think it's telling that God's first words to humans were "You are free" (Genesis 2:16 NIV). Eden was untamed and people were free. The future held forth the promise of infinite challenge, exploration, and adventure. We call Eden a garden, but I think it was more like a jungle. Each moment was a new frontier. Adam and Eve enjoyed both freedom without restraint and happiness without limits. Try to wrap your mind around that. I've tried, and I can't.

Life hummed with harmony just as God had intended it to. Our first parents were in tune with nature and in touch with each other and at peace with the Creator of it all.

I can hardly imagine a place where freedom and happiness are both boundless and don't cancel each other out the way they do in our world. We just can't seem to have one without the other. Not even our best novelists and movie directors have been able to picture that kind of world. In Eden, freedom and happiness complemented each other. They met. They held hands. They ran together through the jungle.[1]

No shame back then; just harmony. Adam and Eve experienced both the elusive happiness and the ultimate freedom we all crave. They lived in the place our greatest saints and holy men have only dreamed about. They immersed themselves in the life our mystics and madmen and prophetesses have only glimpsed in fleeting moments.

It was pure poetry back then. Everything was in sync. And the game was never meant to end.

Yet even here on this early page of our story a shadow looms on the edge of paradise. Evil has slithered onto the scene.

The strings that played the most perfect melody between God and humanity are about to be plucked and snapped in half, and the ancient song would not be heard again until it echoed from an empty grave.

ꙮ

when i pause long enough to listen,
i hear noise rather than music in my soul.
the chords of my heart strain to find the first harmony.
it's there, somewhere in my distant memories,
    i hear snatches of it sometimes
    in the silences, in the corners, on the outskirts of my dreams.
but my days are all so busy and
my moments are all so heavy,
that they pull my hope down again into minor key.
is harmony even possible anymore
in this out of whack, out of tune world?

lead me into the music again.
show me where the breeze of your harmony blows.
    for only with your help
will i ever be part of the original song
again.

orchestration.

what kind of backward flute is this?
what kind of ancient tune do i hear?
rather than charm the snake,
the snake has charmed me.

꙳

Now the serpent was the shrewdest of all the creatures the LORD God
had made. "Really?" he asked the woman. "Did God really say you
must not eat any of the fruit in the garden?"

—*the devil tempting Eve in the Garden of Eden (Genesis 3:1)*

Some people say the old story about Adam and Eve and the snake in
the Garden is just a fable. And I have to admit, it does kind of sound
like one.

You remember the story, don't you? God warns Adam and Eve about
the tree, and despite his warning (or maybe because of it), Eve finds
herself beneath its branches, admiring the forbidden fruit. Enter the
snake tempting Eve. Throw in a few subtle lies: "You won't die if you eat
it! Your eyes will be opened, you'll be like God!" Add a touch of doubt
and desire and allurement and then . . . she plucks . . . she eats . . . she
shares with Adam, indeed their eyes are opened to evil just as the snake
promised, their hearts are stung with the venom of shame and things
are never the same again.

You probably heard the story in Sunday school as a kid or maybe saw
it being made fun of on late night TV.

So is it supposed to be true or metaphorical? Was there really a garden? A literal talking snake? Or is this just a cautionary tale with a mythic message explaining who we are and how we came to be the way we are?

Theologians of all stripes have their explanations. Skeptics have a field day with the talking snake bit. But I'll be honest here: I've seen this story of enticement and shame played out so many times in so many ways with so many people—on college campuses and in nightclubs, in hotel lobbies and coffee shops, in boardrooms and bedrooms—that I don't really question it anymore. I can see how true it is. Whether this story is history or myth, it's true. There's no denying that. It happens all the time. It's not just their story; it's ours as well.

Once after I swallowed a delicious slice of venomous fruit, I wrote this:

> i could leap over the sky
> and float through the stars
>
> if only i weren't weighed down
> with this thing called regret.

But I am weighed down. We all are. Because we continue to pluck and bite and eat. There's nothing as tempting as a "Keep Out" sign and nothing as seductive as the lure of the forbidden. But then afterward, once we've tasted the fruit, shame and guilt ride into town again and the whole nasty business starts all over. We're pathetically predictable that way. We convince ourselves it'll be okay, we'll never get caught, it's no big deal; but then when we do get caught, guilt shatters the harmony just as surely today as it did back then. Adam and Eve fled and God came looking for them, and we've been fleeing and he's been looking ever since.

If I've learned anything at all from the times I've wandered into the realm of the forbidden, it's this: there's always a price to be paid when you listen to the snake. There's always a consequence from biting the fruit. It's cost me friendships, caused me humiliation, gotten me speeding tickets, given me hangovers, and at one point in my life almost cost me my marriage. I know I'm splintered. I'm not the person I should be. None of us are.

In the tragic aftermath of their choice, Adam and Eve's eyes were opened, and they saw for the first time that the harmony was gone. They had to leave the Garden because they were no longer living in tune with their Creator. They'd gone their own way, and each of us has followed. Here's what God told Adam:

> Because you listened to your wife
> and ate from the tree
> That I commanded you not to eat from,
> "Don't eat from this tree,"
> The very ground is cursed because of you;
> getting food from the ground
> Will be as painful as having babies is for your wife;
> you'll be working in pain all your life long.
> The ground will sprout thorns and weeds,
> you'll get your food the hard way,
> Planting and tilling and harvesting,
> sweating in the fields from dawn to dusk,
> Until you return to that ground yourself, dead and buried;
> you started out as dirt, you'll end up dirt.
>
> Genesis 3:17–19 Message

Pain. Death. Sweat. Toil. Thorns. That was one sweeping curse. This tale of choices and rebellion and excuses and shame is replayed over and over in our lives. This journey from lost to found is still being told today. This is our story. Yours and mine.

Here's how the apostle Paul summarized it: "Against its will, everything on earth was subjected to God's curse. All creation anticipates the day when it will join God's children in glorious freedom from death and decay. For we know that all creation has been groaning as in the pains of childbirth right up to the present time" (Romans 8:20–22). Our world is groaning to be set free from death. Our souls are groaning to be set free from the curse.

> a bead of sweat on a glistening forehead.
> knuckles scraped,
> muscles hard and weary,
> skin cut and bruised, caught with splinters,
> feet aching, stumbling, tripping,
> battling back the thorns, the weeds of another day.
> who is this farmer, reaping in his fields?
> this shepherd, gathering his sheep?
> this carpenter, preparing a place?
> who is this man?
>> sitting in traffic surrounded by fumes and angry faces,
>> yelling into a phone,
>> wiping the sweat from his brow,
> deadlines, reports, meetings,
> "just some time with the kids,"
> who is this man in the mirror?
>
> i hardly recognize him anymore.

֍

And so a curse settled down around all of Eve's children. The harmony stopped as abruptly as a CD when you drive over a speed bump. The winds of change blew and brought with them the smell of death. Work became toil. Laughter turned to tears. Joy faded away. The harmony was gone and thorns began to grow, for part of the curse was the prick of the thorn.

But God didn't take away the rose.

In the same breath as the curse, God gave his children a promise of someone to come who would restore harmony again. God told the snake, "From now on, you and the woman will be enemies, and your offspring and her offspring will be enemies. He will crush your head, and you will strike his heel" (Genesis 3:15).

This enigmatic prophecy was the only bright spot on that otherwise dark day. God promised that evil would one day be crushed. The curse would one day be lifted.

And since then, beauty and pain have grown in our world side by side. Suffering and joy exist on the same vine, and tears can taste either bitter or sweet. The thorns weren't a bully-God's way of getting back at those who wouldn't listen to him, they were simply a reminder of who we are. Their prick reminds us who we became on that day when our first parents charted a course away from God and shipwrecked us here on this imperfect island of The Way Things Are.

All their descendants since have scanned the horizon for glimpses of another shore. Some have seen it. Most of us haven't. All of us, though—all of us—perish in this place of pain and death and suffering. The thorns pierce deeply here—thorns of cancer and old age, of drought and shattered dreams and torn Achilles tendons and tsunamis. We ignore them until they prick us and the drop of blood reminds us, *"You are mortal. You can bleed, and one day soon, you will die."*

But God didn't take away the rose.

Generations came and went, and pain followed them everywhere. Death tracked them down one at a time; tracks us down one at a time. Pain in birth, pain in life, pain in death. And though some people point to pain as evidence that God doesn't exist or simply doesn't care about us anymore, I think pain is really the evidence of our evil, not his.

> Then Pilate had Jesus flogged with a lead-tipped whip. The soldiers made a crown of long, sharp thorns and put it on his head, and they put a royal purple robe on him. "Hail! King of the Jews!" they mocked, and they hit him with their fists.
>
> John 19:1–3

The fists that beat Jesus were formed by human hands, that lead-tipped whip was wielded by a human will—hands just as human as ours, a will just as hardened as Adam's. The crown of thorns was woven by human fingers, not God's.

Our first parents chose the path of rebellion. They chose the knowledge of good *and evil.* And the only way to know evil is to experience it firsthand. The harsh and hateful truth is that we've known it all too well ever since.

But God didn't take away the rose.

᛭

the stars are slow in singing to me tonight.
"who has broken your lyre?" i ask.
"who has scattered your voices?"

and then i hear the answer deep within me;
echoing along the shores of my heart. . . .
and it's my own name that i hear.
so finally, i understand:
    i am the one the stars are ashamed of.

all because of what i've become
going my own way,
charting my own course
so far away from you.
    so very far away.

forgive me for the whole fruit-incident.
i know its juice is still fresh on my lips.

mutiny.

blood pours through my veins,
giving me life.
my head and heart and soul
are full of blood.

maybe that's why i have
such bloody thoughts, bloody desires,
bloody dreams.

☙

Then the LORD said to Cain, "Why are you angry? Why is your face downcast? If you do what is right, will you not be accepted? But if you do not do what is right, sin is crouching at your door; it desires to have you, but you must master it."

—*God's warning to Cain when he became jealous of his younger brother Abel (Genesis 4:6–7 NIV)*

"What is it, Cain? What do you want?"

Abel had repeated the question twice now, and I still hadn't answered. I just stared at him, wondering if I could really do it, if I could really carry it out. So many thoughts were racing through my mind. *He's your brother, Cain . . . God warned you about your anger . . . You don't have to do this . . .*

But then, another voice.

Who does God think he is, telling me what to do? I'll do what I want to do!

"Cain?"

And then I remembered how it felt when I first had the idea. It was like a chill that passes over you when the wind blows across your face at night. Except this time the chill stayed. *Everything dies, Cain. The sheep, the birds . . . You're just helping things along . . .*

"Cain, are you okay?"

"There's something I want to talk to you about," I said finally.

"Yes?"

"Not here. Let's go for a walk, over there, in the field."

Abel glanced at the fertile floodplain and then back at me. He paused for a moment and then shrugged. "Okay, whatever."

He doesn't suspect a thing!

I led him toward the tall grasses that would hide everything. *They'll keep your secret*, I told myself. *No one will ever find out!*

Still, I wasn't sure if I could actually do it. I mean, I'd killed animals before. I knew what that was like. I knew how their bodies twitched and stiffened and slowly cooled, then warmed again and began to stink in the aftermath of death. I didn't know if it would be the same for people. No one had ever died before.

Sharp brambles bit into my hands and legs like teeth as we entered the field, drawing blood. No surprise there. It seems like thorns are growing everywhere these days. Abel was saying something about his flock of stupid sheep, but I wasn't listening. I was leading him somewhere specific.

I was only a step or two in front of him. Only a few more feet. Then he placed his hand on my shoulder. "Cain, what is it? Where are we going? What did you want to talk to me about?"

In answer I bent down and grabbed the rock. I knew right where it'd be. I'd put it there earlier in the day. It was about the size of a goat's head; I figured that would be big enough. In one smooth motion I stood, raising the rock above my head and turning toward him. Abel stared at me curiously. He didn't seem to understand what was going on, what the wickedly jagged rock was for.

Then, right before I brought it down as hard as I could against his skull, fear clouded his face. The last thing my brother knew was terror.

As the rock connected with his head, I heard a deep crunch, somehow moist and solid at the same time. The force of the blow snapped his head awkwardly to the right, twisting his whole body around. He landed with a dull thud on the dark, rich soil, his body twitching slightly.

I walked over to him.

Make sure, a voice told me. *Make sure he's dead.*

I stood above him and looked into his eyes. They looked different. Faraway, distant, unfocused. Maybe that's what death was like—losing focus forever. My heart was racing, my head spinning.

So this is what it feels like to kill a man, I thought. *Finish him! Finish him!*

I raised the rock and brought it down against his face. I had to do it three or four times before the twitching stopped for good. Then everything was silent except for the distant cry of a few crows. And all was still except for the growing pool of thick, dark blood seeping slowly into the earth.

❧

Afterward the LORD asked Cain, "Where is your brother? Where is Abel?"

"I don't know!" Cain retorted. "Am I supposed to keep track of him wherever he goes?"

But the LORD said, "What have you done? Listen—your brother's blood cries out to me from the ground!"

Genesis 4:9–10

After the harmony was shattered and Adam and Eve had to leave Eden, Eve had two sons. But the divine image God had imprinted on humanity's soul had become marred forever. The boys resembled their father more than their Father. And as they grew, they just couldn't seem to get along. Jealousy and bitterness and resentment and hatred wormed their way into Cain's heart. Sin rang his doorbell, and he threw open the door and invited it in for dinner and a movie.

It didn't take long for blood to stain the pages of our story. And it's a stain that has never really washed away.

One day when I was in high school my parents left me home alone with my younger brother while they ran errands. I was supposed to watch him. Well, we argued about something dumb, I have no idea what, and in a rage I rushed into the kitchen and grabbed a knife—not a butter knife but one of those horror movie knives designed for slicing meat from bone.

I stood there shaking, the knife blade reflecting back a distorted, angular version of my face. I had a choice. I could either set down the knife and go outside to shoot baskets, or I could walk into the living room and stab my little brother in the chest.

A moment later I finally came to my senses. I dropped the knife onto the table, where its clatter echoed like high-pitched laughter. I escaped into my room, my heart jackhammering in my chest, scared of what I could have so easily done, so easily become.

My dad told me that when he was a kid, his brother hit him in the head with a hammer.

As I write this, thousands of people in Darfur, Sudan, are being systematically massacred and starved to death each week by the Sudanese government. The United Nations has criticized it but hasn't taken any definitive steps to stop it. Just over a decade ago, more than 800,000 people were murdered in Rwanda, most of them cut to pieces with machetes, before anyone stepped in to stop the slaughter.

In the twentieth century, one out of every twenty-two human deaths was caused by another human.[1]

☙

can poison taste of nectar?
can venom taste of wine?
yes, for we have licked the fruit and plucked it from the vine.
yes, for we have tasted evil, succulent and sweet,
and passed it on for others,
to lick, and taste,
and eat.

Anger and envy still infect our relationships. Hatred still haunts us. Violence still stalks us. This whole story of Cain's nosedive into evil is chillingly familiar. Evil still crouches at the door, ready to pounce. We hear the doorbell ring and we rise from the couch to see who's there.

The first human ever born murdered the second. It seems both tragic and ironic to me. But it's not the kind of irony that makes me want to laugh. Not at all.

As time went by, evil grew stronger and stronger in the hearts of men, until finally: "The LORD observed the extent of the people's wickedness, and he saw that all their thoughts were consistently and totally evil. So the LORD was sorry he had ever made them. It broke his heart" (Genesis 6:5–6).

Evil had embedded itself deeply into the human story.

When I'm honest with myself, I can't keep up the illusion that I'm really a pretty good person. Deep down, coursing through my soul, are the same currents of jealousy and resentment and bitterness and rebellion that surfaced in the life of Cain. The currents flow all throughout our human family, deadly and deep—currents as old as Eden and as thick as blood. And sometimes they bubble to the surface when we least expect it.

ᛣ

touching the unseen

with bloodstained thoughts and a bloodstained heart
i come to you.
    what will it take to wash off these stains?
    what will it take to purge my past?

cain is not just abel's brother.
that much i know.
he is also mine.

guilty.

every fragment of every rainbow
is another echo of light.

when will the final rainbow appear
and glisten at last,

in my soul?

༈

The LORD has sent this message to every land: "Tell the people of
Israel, 'Look, your Savior is coming. See, he brings his reward with
him as he comes.'"

—*God's reminder to his people about his promise and their destiny*
(Isaiah 62:11)

I'm ashamed to admit that I've sometimes offered people cheap hope.
I've made Jesus seem like a backslapping frat buddy rather than a war-
hardened hero. I've peddled him like the peanut guy at the ballpark.
"God! I've got some red-hot God here!"

I've held out the plastic, easy hope hyped by the preachers of a bargain-
basement God when all the while, the hope God offers is raw and real
and unvarnished. It rises through the centuries and reverberates in the

hearts and souls of true spiritual pilgrims everywhere. This is not a cheap hope but a costly one. It's a tearstained hope strong enough to comfort people who've watched their parents die, seen their dreams fade away, struggled with whether or not to have an abortion, or lived through a divorce. It's a hope for the oppressed, the guilty, the haunted, the hurting, the forgotten, the abused, the mocked, the ignored, the lonely, and the overlooked. Workaholics and loudmouths and outcasts and spiritual fugitives like us.

It's a passionate hope, a real hope, a battle-scarred and yet victorious hope. Only a hope like that could ever conquer heartaches this strong and wounds this deep and pain as fresh as today's headlines.

⁂

After Cain and Abel, the Easter narrative spins off in two distinct directions, one of shadow, one of light. The two stories curl around each other, intertwining like yin and yang. Like an M. C. Escher painting. At first they look like they're embracing each other, but when you look closer, you see that really light is chasing shadow toward an empty tomb.

The shadowy side of the saga is humanity's descent into darkness. Choice after choice, generation after generation, evil has seeped deeper and deeper into the souls of everyday women and men.

The tale of light is the thread of God's graciousness extended over and over to a people who turned their backs on him. When their wickedness got out of hand, he gave them 120 years to get their act together. But they chose not to. So then came Noah and the Really Big Houseboat. But when the great flood had receded, it didn't take long for people to fumble the ball all over again.

They built a tower in honor of themselves, and God had to scatter them across the globe the hard way, obstinate people that we are. At last he chose a man of faith named Abram (later renamed Abraham). For reasons of his own, God decided to pour his promises into the world through this elderly, childless nomad. Both Jews and Arabs trace their ancestry back to Abraham. And in time, the Jews became the people of God's promises.

God told Abraham, "I will bless you richly. I will multiply your descendants into countless millions, like the stars of the sky and the sand on the seashore. They will conquer their enemies, and through your descendants, all the nations of the earth will be blessed" (Genesis 22:17–18). All the nations would be blessed through this nation and through one of Abraham's descendants—a man with the power to restore hope to all of humanity.

Then God sealed his promise and instituted an intricate system of sacrifices to remind his people of his promises. Each lamb that was slaughtered, each dove that was slain, each drop of blood that was sprinkled on a desert altar was another arrow pointing into the future to the fulfillment of God's promises: he would be with them, he would never abandon them, and in time, he would rescue them.

God called his chosen people his bride, but their hearts went in search of other lovers. Those fractured souls in need of love sneered at their lover's advances and pursued one-night stands instead. To God every act of idolatry was an act of spiritual adultery. So their story was, so our story is.

lover of my soul, i've been unfaithful.

flirting with the lurid promises
of fortune and glory and passion and fame,
of lust and pride and greed and comfort.
i've followed them into the bedroom
    where i think no one will find me.
    where i hope you're not watching.
    where we live out our fantasies together.
i've slept in the arms of so many lovers
but they've left me hollowed out,
a corpse and an empty casing tumbling in the wind.

i've cheated on you again and again.
in the red-light district of my soul.

God had whispered his first promise to Adam and Eve in those early days of creation and rebellion. Now throughout the years he repeated it in a variety of ways to a variety of people. With each retelling through the centuries, the promise took on more clarity, more specificity, more wonder, more mystery.

A Savior would arrive . . . a serpent-slayer . . . a deliverer . . . a king whose kingdom would never end . . . a servant who would suffer for his people . . . a prophet who would speak for God . . . a priest who would offer the final and ultimate sacrifice . . . a man who would bring blessing to all the races of people on earth. Chapter after chapter of the Old Testament retells the tale, clarifies the promises, resounds the echo: "The people who walk in darkness will see a great light—a light that will shine on all who live in the land where death casts its shadow" (Isaiah 9:2).

And each promise, each prediction, each prophecy shed more light and more mystery on this figure: He would be God; he would be a man. He would be a king; he would be a servant. He would be both a lion and a lamb, both a sword and a shield, both a conqueror and the conquered one. The prophet Isaiah called him, "Wonderful Counselor, Mighty God, Everlasting Father, Prince of Peace" (Isaiah 9:6). And the hope he would bring would not be cheap but as costly as life itself and as bright as the rising sun.

But how could this be? And who would this be? And when would he finally arrive?

They dreamt of him. They longed for him. They spoke of him from generation to generation. At mealtimes and around campfires and along lonely desert journeys, they told of him. Promises of his coming echoed through their days. Every ritual, every prayer, every prophecy was another reminder.

But he didn't come. That's the thing. Year after year they waited, but the promised one didn't arrive.

⸓

touching the unseen

deep in the center of dawn
the echo returns.
floating on the edge of your words
i hear hope circling around my heart
    "soon, soon, the savior will arrive.
    soon, soon, the king will come."
when will you arrive and show me
the way out of this maze
of myself? i'm feeling more and more lost
every moment i'm here.

splintered.

chains

i am drowning in awareness,
and yet never quite aware
that the chains i fashion every day
are the very ones i wear.

🙟

Some sat in darkness and deepest gloom,
miserable prisoners in chains.
They rebelled against the words of God,
scorning the counsel of the Most High.
That is why he broke them with hard labor;
they fell, and no one helped them rise again.

*—an anonymous songwriter, exploring the desperate
condition of God's people (Psalm 107:10–12)*

I heard a story about a king whose brother tried unsuccessfully to assassinate him. As punishment, the king imprisoned his brother in a room with a window facing the sea. The room had a normal-sized door that a normal-sized person could walk through. They must have built the room around the guy, though, because the king's brother wasn't normal-sized at all—he was way overweight.

So all he had to do to be free was lose enough weight to fit through the door. But every day the king's servants brought platters of fine food to him. They set the food in the window. That was his sentence—overcome his addiction or die in that cell.

And he died in that cell.

Just as the king knew he would.

And the person in the story I can identify with most is that imprisoned brother, staring at the gulls and the open water, eating another mouthful of rich food and telling himself that tomorrow he'll deal with his problem and walk out the door. Yeah, he'll start tomorrow. Or someday. Whichever comes first.

But neither ever did.

⳨

Through Abraham and his descendants, God's promises traveled throughout the Middle East until they landed in Egypt, in the hearts of the Israelites. But in time, "The Egyptians made the Israelites their slaves and put brutal slave drivers over them, hoping to wear them down under heavy burdens" (Exodus 1:11).

In the ensuing enslavement, God orchestrated the birth and training of a boy who would become a powerful deliverer. His name: Moses. He grew up in the palace, then spent a good chunk of his life in exile as a shepherd after killing an abusive Egyptian guard. God chose this fugitive to set his people free. I think maybe God chose a murderer to lead his people so no one could ever accuse the Almighty of playing favorites.

When Moses returned to Egypt after encountering God at the burning bush, he had fire in his eyes and miracles in his hands. The plagues came quickly then: water turning into blood . . . frogs . . . locusts . . . hail . . . darkness . . .

Each plague more devastating than the last; each plague stronger than the corresponding gods the Egyptians worshiped. Hopi, the god of the Nile, couldn't stop the water from turning into blood; the frog goddess Heqt couldn't stop the infestation of frogs; Apis, the bull god, and Hathor, the goddess of cows, couldn't stop boils from growing on the bovines; the revered sun god Re couldn't remove the darkness.

It made Pharaoh insane with rage. *How could this scraggly, stuttering shepherd bring mighty Egypt to its knees? How! How could his God be so strong?*

So Pharaoh refused Moses's request to free the Hebrews, and he wouldn't acknowledge Moses's God. After all, he didn't want to lose his Israelite slaves. But as anyone who's ever fought with God can tell you, God doesn't lose, and he doesn't surrender.

So then the final plague came. A ghastly judgment on a land of people who'd hardened their hearts, a people whose hard hearts were about to be broken.

God's instructions to the Jews were these: kill a one-year-old lamb with no deformities and smear the blood on the door frames of your home. Then roast the meat with bitter herbs and serve it with bread without yeast. Dress for a trip and eat quickly, because deliverance is on its way.

Okay, I admit, it's a bit weird. But there was a deeper significance to the lamb's blood. God was weaving a tale that would make sense much later, on a dewy dawn by an empty tomb. But for now, here's what God told his people:

> The blood you have smeared on your doorposts will serve as a sign. When I see the blood, I will pass over you. This plague of death will not touch you when I strike the land of Egypt. You must remember this day forever. Each year you will celebrate it as a special festival to the LORD.
>
> Exodus 12:13–14

That night, not a single Egyptian home was spared. The firstborn sons died, and the grief-stricken mothers wailed. Yet the Hebrew families were saved because of the blood of the lambs.

God's judgment passed over his people. The blood on their door frames mapped the movement of his grace through the land. And this yearly celebration of the lamb and the blood became the backbone of the Jewish festival calendar—a meal called the Passover.

The two threads continued to intertwine: darkness and light, rebellion and grace, pain and deliverance.

☧

what do i need in my life
to keep the shrieking at bay?

what do i need to do
to get your anger to pass
over me?

The next day the Hebrews began their desert journey toward the Promised Land, but along the way their faith faltered. Their newfound freedom became laced with blood and treachery. Compromise, unbelief, and idolatry swayed their hearts. They left the land of slavery, but they took their chains along. A shadow had ensnared their souls.

In their hearts and ours is a deeper slavery, a stronger chain than any Egyptian slave driver could wield. Sometimes others enslave us, but most of the time we're the ones who enslave ourselves. Choice after choice. Bite after bite of forbidden fruit. *Someday I'll overcome this and be free,* we tell ourselves. *Someday.*

Jesus put it this way: "I assure you that everyone who sins is a slave of sin. A slave is not a permanent member of the family, but a son is part of the family forever. So if the Son sets you free, you will indeed be free" (John 8:34–36). Sinners become enslaved by their sins. And freedom can only come through Jesus.

God knew about those fatal chains on our souls, stretching back to a choice in a garden. And he had a plan to snap them once and for all by sending his Son.

God knows all about our addictions to power and pride and gambling and pornography and cocaine and depression and anger and Cheetos. He knows how quick we are to hold grudges and how slow we are to forgive. He knows about our tendency to worship what we create. He knows how much we like to take what isn't ours, say what isn't true, distort the truth to our advantage, take credit for what we haven't done, have our way at any cost, belittle those who disagree with us, step on those who get in our way, evade, excuse, attack, justify, rationalize, indulge in our fantasies, and look for loopholes.

Paul explained our condition like this: "Don't you know that when you offer yourselves to someone to obey him as slaves, you are slaves to the one whom you obey—whether you are slaves to sin, which leads to death, or to obedience, which leads to righteousness?" (Romans 6:16 NIV).

Every choice we make forges another invisible link on yet another internal chain that leads either toward freedom or death, toward heaven or hell.

You can't tell the history of Israel without mentioning chains. You can't tell the history of humanity without mentioning blood and terror and longing and slavery. And you'll never understand Easter without first seeing the chains in your own heart.

Here is the paradox of the thing we call *freedom*: the farther we wander from God and the more we try to break free from him, the more enchained we become. Every step we take away from him leads us farther from the freedom of Jesus and closer to the cruelty of Cain.

Whips and fists and tears and chains are the chapter headings of the human story—a story that's still unfolding, still being told. A tale in which darkness is alive, and hell is all too often at high tide.

But there's one thing stronger than the chains on our souls: the love of a Jewish carpenter.

The crack of dawn at Easter was really the sound of chains falling away.

⁂

touching the unseen

i'm a caged bird,
rattling the bars of my cage
with furious flutterings.

break my chains!
free my spirit!
let me fly with the wings you have
drawn upon my soul
with heaven-dipped ink.

dusk is fast approaching.
where are you?
when will you come to
smash the lock upon my heart
and free me, at last,
from myself?

i am my own prison
and you are the only key.

enslaved.

can something be both as solid as stone and as hollow as an echo?
only one thing.

what's that?
a human heart.

⚜

God has made everything beautiful for its own time. He has planted
eternity in the human heart, but even so, people cannot see the
whole scope of God's work from beginning to end.

—*King Solomon, reflecting on the paradox of our immortal hungers
and our limited understanding (Ecclesiastes 3:11)*

Television commercials annoy me. They're always telling me my car
isn't sporty enough, my breath isn't fresh enough, my armpits aren't dry
enough, my investments aren't secure enough, my teeth aren't bright
enough, my beer isn't filling enough, and my insurance company isn't
cheap enough—and that I'll be cooler, happier, hipper, more popular,
pain free, and handsome if I just chew their brand of gum, use their
brand of athlete's foot cream, and wipe my rump with their brand of
squeezably soft toilet paper.

One night I saw a commercial for this really big, juicy cheeseburger,
and I was sitting there thinking, *Man, that looks good. I oughtta just slip
out and go get one.* So I grabbed my shoes and was lacing them up when
another commercial came on from a different restaurant chain telling

me how much saturated fat that first commercial's burgers had. I stopped lacing up my shoes. *Man, that's nasty.*

None of the commercials have to convince me that I don't have enough joy, peace, freedom, love, friendship, or satisfaction in my life. The advertisers just take that for granted. In fact, they put a magnifying glass up to my longings and then offer me solutions both of us know won't work. That's the kicker.

And the worst part about it is that I keep watching their commercials. I keep buying their stuff. I keep hoping that maybe they're right after all, that all these deep nagging desires will finally go away if I use their product—that happiness really will come from a can of shaving cream or a tube of toothpaste.

If this world of chalupas and dandruff shampoo and Viagra is all there is, how come I have hungers that none of those things ever seem to satisfy? The mystic Sundar Singh wrote, "Thirst is an expression of our need for water and a sign of hope that somewhere there is water that can satisfy our thirst. Similarly, the deep longing in our soul is a clear sign of hope that spiritual peace exists."[1]

We don't feed a hungry man sawdust or give a thirsty man a pillow. That's not what he needs. So why do we try to fill our hunger for the mysterious, the spiritual, the eternal with cognac, ecstasy, reality shows, affairs, and chicken fajitas?

We tell ourselves that this meal, this promotion, this drug, this one-night stand will finally make us happy. But they don't because they can't. It's the wrong food. We're feeling our way around a dark room, groping for a happiness that's always out of reach. If only we would take the time to turn on the light, we'd see how empty the room really is. We're looking in the wrong place.

Jesus once said, "People need more than bread for their life; they must feed on every word of God" (Matthew 4:4). If we're not feeding on the words of God, a great big part of our souls will be starving. Most people never devour the life-giving words that would help them to finally be born. If we never nourish our lives through a spiritual connection with God, we'll remain achingly hungry for mystery, transcendence, and a real relationship with the almighty.

The ancient Israelites had soul longings too. They longed for a return to Eden just as much as we do today. And because of God's promises, they tied their longings to the coming of a great deliverer: "In that day the heir to David's throne will be a banner of salvation to all the world. The nations will rally to him, for the land where he lives will be a glorious place" (Isaiah 11:10). They longed for that glorious place. Yet the Old Testament is the tragic record of how they tried to fill their soul longings time after time with the wrong kind of food.

⅟

I dreamt, and in my dream an angel appeared to me, hovering just out of reach.

"Tell me about your world," she said.

"Well, it's a good world," I said. "A wonderful place, actually, where healing can be found in even the deepest of our wounds . . . and yet . . ."

"And yet?"

"Yet it's a painful and pain-filled world where scars appear on the souls of even the greatest of our saints."

"Your world is a mystery!" said the angel.

"Yes."

"And have you tried to be good? To make your world a better place?"

"Yes," I said. "Of course. We've tried over and over. And we've failed. Over and over. So we tell ourselves that trying to be good is good enough, even though we know it's not. And we tell ourselves to *feel* good, even though we know we are not good."

"So you live an illusion?"

I paused. "I guess so, although I've never really thought of it like that."

"Has it worked?"

I shook my head. "No. But we don't dare admit it. Instead, we tell ourselves that it'll most certainly work next time . . . if only we try harder."

"But even your saints are failures?"

"They're the ones most aware of their failings and the first to admit them. The rest of us claim we're good even though we're not. And our saints claim they aren't good even though they are. We think of the saints as holy, but they see themselves only as unclean and in need of healing."

"So, your sickest spirits think they are well and your healthiest souls know they are sick?"

"I guess so."

"You live in a puzzling world, indeed!"

"To us it doesn't seem puzzling or mysterious. To us, it seems normal and dull and tiresome—"

"—and sad?"

"Yes. And sad. Very sad."

"Isn't there any hope for your world?"

I didn't know what to say. "We hope there's hope, but we're not sure. This much we do know: any hope won't come from within our world or from within our hearts because—"

"—even your saints have stains on their souls."

"Yes. Even our saints."

And then, we were both silent for a long time. I didn't want to open my mouth again. Everything I told her made me sadder.

Finally, with a flutter of light, she was gone. But before she left, she touched me with the tips of her wings, and my heart still burns with the memory of her, even today.

꙳

Here's what I've discovered about myself: my hunger for the eternal is maddening when I leave God out of the picture. Without God in the equation, I'm left only with a confusing pile of piercing longings and nothing real to connect them to.

I think even those who've never heard of Eden long for it. If we knew that "happily ever after" were only true in fairy tales, we'd give up hope. But instead we tell ourselves there must be more to life. There *must* be! This hope for a brighter future and a better tomorrow is what compels us to get up in the morning and keeps us from committing suicide at night.

And yet in this world we find disappointment after disappointment. We bite into the chocolate bunny over and over again and find it's hollow each and every time.

Year after year and generation after generation, we tirelessly tell ourselves that there's a reason to hope, that this thing called life will have a happy ending. If we don't keep telling ourselves this, we end up with a razor blade pressed against our wrists, thinking dark and final thoughts.

Jesus once said, "My purpose is to give life in all its fullness" (John 10:10). And we long for that kind of life, for his words to be real—as real as a cup of espresso or a stack of clean laundry. We want our soul hungers to be satisfied. We want God's whispered promises to come true. The Old Testament tells the saga of the Jewish nation, a longing nation. A nation of people just like us with longings as old as Eden and as fresh as the dew on Easter morning.

֍

touching the unseen

you seem so far away from me today.
just out of reach.
or maybe i'm the one who's out of reach.
out of touch.
what is it in me that makes you so hard to see?
i need new eyes. spiritual eyeballs that look past
    the bills that need paying
    and the car that needs fixing
    and the e-mails that keep coming
to see what lies beyond.
eyes that can see in the dark.
and through the dark
to you.

i've been looking
in the wrong place all this time—
    in myself rather than in you,
    within this world rather than
    beyond it where the kingdom
    of God resides, where you live,
    and secretly smile at my shortsightedness—
    and wait.
i'm glad you're so patient.

quest.

prophets yell because
their hearts are on fire.

they scream at the world
trying to wake us up.

they can't help it.
after all,
God is in their throats.

᷍

O God, don't sit idly by,
silent and inactive!
Don't you hear the tumult of your enemies?
Don't you see what your arrogant enemies are doing?

—the opening lines of a wartime prayer by Asaph
(Psalm 83:1–2)

The Savior didn't come.

The years passed, the echo of the promises faded away, and the long-ings remained. Israel's perennial enemies thrived, and the Savior didn't come. God's people watched for him. They waited for him. They prayed and sacrificed and worshiped and dutifully flipped their calendars. And God answered all their longings with silence.

For many of them, the dream of harmony became harder and harder to hear beneath the noise of the years and the cries of their nagging doubts.

Some stopped listening altogether. And with each passing year, more of God's children gave up believing. The dream lost its footing in their souls, and the echo of God's promise became thinner and fainter in their lives.

It seemed so much safer and saner to stay there on the seashore of reason than to chance the waves and enter the sea of faith. So God's children became rational, realistic, reasonable, practical, pragmatic people who abandoned faith for sight and traded worship for religion. Over and over again they chose the knowledge of evil and the juicy fruit of the forbidden until hope itself began to fade away.

> when i was young i drank cases and cases of dreams
> because that was all i could afford. and it was the only
> thing my grocer kept in stock.
> but i never became drunk,
> because i didn't learn how to swallow them
> deeply enough.

⸙

For nearly a dozen centuries, God's people, the Israelites, were caught in a cycle. They would listen to God for a while, follow him, worship him, call out to him, and then they'd drift away from him all over again. It wasn't a conscious thing. It never is. They just became more and more entangled in their own goals and involved in their own lives, easing into compromise, ambition, and success.

And then during their times of prosperity and comfort, they became complacent. And forgetful. They let God's story slip from their hearts as they pursued their own stories instead. They forgot to call on his name as they became distracted by making a name for themselves.

So God sent thorns of various names and shapes and sizes to prick them from their spiritual slumber and awaken them to his presence. He let them wander in the desert, he let their stomachs growl with hunger, he let their throats ache with thirst, he let their enemies oppress them, he let venomous snakes bite them, he let the clouds hold back the rain, and all the while, with angry voices and blunt words, the prophets and prophetesses bludgeoned the consciences of the Israelites. God's spokesmen and spokeswomen tried to shake them up, to wake them up. But for the most part, it didn't work. The Israelites turned away from God. "They forgot God, their savior, who had done such great things in Egypt" (Psalm 106:21).

God coaxed them with his promises, he clobbered them with his threats, but still they wouldn't turn back wholeheartedly to him. Even when he forgave them, restored them, protected them, and rescued them, they rejected him all over again, their souls fast asleep to his presence.

As in a fairy tale, they slept. Season after season, encircled by thorns. Sometimes they awakened for a brief moment and changed their ways and returned to their first love for a while, but then, all too soon, they closed their eyes once again and dozed off as the thorns encircled them and tightened around their hearts. The curse was winning.

‡

Every generation has had people who have questioned whether or not God is real, but few people have ever questioned whether or not God is silent. There's not a whole lot of question about that. God's silence is all too real. It's a deafening roar in our souls. Martyrs die whispering his name and receiving only death in response to their faith. Children helplessly watch their parents lose touch with reality through Alzheimer's, begging God for a miracle that never comes.

Where is God in those times? Why is he so silent? If God really loves us with an everlasting love, with an unfailing and enduring and magnificent love, then shouldn't he be more visible? Shouldn't he splinter the silence more often?

Welcome to the riddle of the universe.

King David, the person God called "a man after his own heart" (1 Samuel 13:14), wrote these words: "My God, my God! Why have you forsaken me? Why do you remain so distant? Why do you ignore my cries for help?" (Psalm 22:1).

And you may remember Jesus echoing those words 1030 years later when he yelled them from the cross: "My God, my God, why have you forsaken me?" (Matthew 27:46).

It's such a big question, even Jesus didn't know the answer.

When a man named Job asked God why all the bad stuff was happening in his life, God was silent for thirty-seven chapters of the Bible. Finally God told him, "Who are you to question me?" And Job shut up rather quickly (see Job 38–40).

We yearn for God's presence. We call to him. We scream at him. And we hear nothing. He answers our longings with silence. Sometimes his silence is unbearable—especially for those who choose to keep believing in him.

These words were found scrawled on the wall of a concentration camp:

I believe in the sun, even though it doesn't shine,
I believe in love, even when it isn't shown,
I believe in God, even when he doesn't speak.[1]

God's silence offers us the choice—faith or sight. We can either abandon our faith or learn to trust in the dark. God leaves that choice up to us. And all the while he's more interested in our faith in him than our ability to decipher his silences. The poet Coleman Barks wrote, "The only way we *know* the play of destiny and free will is to dance the mystery and die inside it."[2]

Jesus, Job, David, and that man in the concentration camp danced the mystery.

I can't think of a single place in the whole Bible where God actually explained his silence. I can think of lots of times when people asked him to, but I'm not sure he ever did. I don't know why God is so silent. I really don't know. I do know that none of those men—David, Jesus, or Job—gave up on God. And God never gave up on them.

When you listen to a song, you only hear the harmony because of the emptiness between the notes. If the song is too full of notes, it becomes nothing but noise. To hear the harmony you have to let the silences have their place in the song. It's like each note is a pearl upon a necklace and the silences are what strings them all together.

Maybe God knows that without his silences in our lives, we will never hear the melody of faith.

I think in every person's life a day comes when faith becomes a choice. You can either give up on the silence of God or choose to trust him in the dark as Jesus did while he was dying on the cross.

In the end, most of the Israelites gave up on God.

And at last, God stopped sending his prophets. He stopped speaking to his people. The Old Testament ends with the word *curse*. And that terrible word echoed in the hearts of his people for four more centuries.

While God remained silent. As silent as the sky.

⁂

love wants to split this moment
into half shells of sweet
almond juice. what's holding
back my soul from opening up to
the song playing, there,
in the light before me?

ah, even fire cannot
stir a soul so fast asleep.

will i ever awaken enough
to taste the juice dripping
out of your promises,
landing soft and gentle on my soul?

asleep.

light

i lick at the light and it soothes the
burning rage of my tongue.

but when it enters my heart,
it sets all of me on fire.

☦

Because of God's tender mercy,
the light from heaven is about to break upon us,
to give light to those who sit in darkness and in the shadow of
death, and to guide us to the path of peace.

—*Zechariah the priest predicting the birth of Jesus of Nazareth*
(Luke 1:78–79)

Early in my marriage I returned home after a four-day trip and from the
moment I walked through the door, my two daughters wouldn't leave
me alone. They clung to my legs, climbed into my arms, and jabbered
about all the things they'd done with Mommy while I was gone.

"Did you miss your daddy?" I ask, just to hear them say that they
did.

"Of course," says my three-year-old. Her sister, a year younger, nods
her head and says, "Me! Me!"

So I play with them for a while and then get ready to tuck the older
girl in bed while her sister gets a bath with Mommy.

I sit next to her on the bed, and she hands me a chunky children's book. "Read the whole book," she says.

"Just a few stories."

But after every story she begs, "One more, Daddy! Pleeeeeeeease?"

I read the whole book.

And then we say prayers, I tell her a story, and I turn on a CD of music for her. I was in a bit of a hurry because I wanted to meet a bunch of my friends at the gym to play basketball.

"Good night," I say, heading to the door.

But she calls to me, "Daddy, will you sleep with me for a little while?"

"What?"

"Sleep with me."

I sigh under my breath and head back to her bed. I sit beside her bed and hold her little pink hand in my own. I'm starting to get really antsy now because I don't want to miss the game, so after a few moments, I figure she's asleep, and I stand up to leave.

I barely make it three steps before she calls to me again.

"Daddy, I'm scared."

"Of what?"

"The dark."

"What dark?"

"The dark up there." She points up at the corner of the room.

So I open the door a little wider and turn to leave.

"Daddy, would you smile at me?"

Smile at her? She wants me to smile at her?

Oh, man.

"Um, yeah," I say, feeling like a heartless ogre. And I go to her bed one last time and smile at her. She smiles back at me again, she closes her eyes, and, clinging to my hand, she goes to sleep.

She had missed me. That was all. And she didn't want to be left alone in the dark.

❧

God broke four hundred years of silence with a birth announcement to a peasant girl from the hill country of Judea. After centuries of waiting and hoping and watching and yearning, after centuries of darkness and doubt and longing, the time had finally come for the deliverer to be born. God opened up the door in heaven to let a little more light into the world. And then he smiled through the night at his children.

> "Don't be frightened, Mary," the angel told her, "for God has decided to bless you! You will become pregnant and have a son, and you are to name him Jesus. He will be very great and will be called the Son of the Most High. And the Lord God will give him the throne of his ancestor David. And he will reign over Israel forever; his Kingdom will never end!"
>
> Mary asked the angel, "But how can I have a baby? I am a virgin."
>
> The angel replied, "The Holy Spirit will come upon you, and the power of the Most High will overshadow you. So the baby born to you will be holy, and he will be called the Son of God. . . ."
>
> Mary responded, "I am the Lord's servant, and I am willing to accept whatever he wants. May everything you have said come true." And then the angel left.
>
> Luke 1:30–35, 38

God chose this Jewish teenage girl to be the mother of humanity's Savior. I love her initial confusion about how she's going to have the baby. She was engaged to a man named Joseph but hadn't slept with him yet—hadn't slept with anyone yet. She couldn't imagine having a baby outside of marriage. Already that tells me a lot about Mary.

And then, when the angel reassured her it was all going to happen according to God's plan and through his power, Mary said yes. She offered herself body and soul to God, even though in her culture unwed pregnant teens could have faced death by stoning.

She said yes, and God's Spirit overshadowed her.

> the almighty overshadowed you—
> bringing you light.
> veiled in Spirit, he wove
> himself through your soul
> whispering life to your womb.
>
> the almighty overshadowed you,
> and the power of his presence
> passed through you,
> and into your Son.
>   and into the world.
> and eventually into me.
> you are my sister in faith and
> the mother of my God.
>
> he overshadowed you
> with the fire of his presence.

☦

For nine months Mary carried the light of the world in the warmth of her womb. And then, in a stable surrounded by a bunch of farm animals, she gave birth to her firstborn son. She lovingly wrapped him in strips of cloth and laid the light of life in the manger. As the apostle John wrote, "Life itself was in him, and this life gives light to everyone. The light shines through the darkness, and the darkness can never extinguish it" (John 1:4–5).

It's so absurd, this king of the galaxies lying in a feed box for animals, this Creator crying in the stable. Anyone can see at this point that this story isn't man-made. Who would ever believe it? If I were making up a religion that I wanted people to believe in, I'd never insert stuff like this. Only God could tell a story this ludicrous and then claim that it is true.

Mary's tiny baby would separate light from darkness. This child would cause a line to be drawn in the sands of eternity and in the hearts of all people everywhere. He would shine into, and then through, the lives of all who would choose to follow him. As Jesus said later, "I am the light of the world. If you follow me, you won't be stumbling through the darkness, because you will have the light that leads to life. . . . I have come as a light to shine in this dark world, so that all who put their trust in me will no longer remain in the darkness" (John 8:12; 12:46) and "Believe in the light while there is still time; then you will become children of the light" (John 12:36).

The words of Jesus have the power to impale the darkness and create offspring of light. Life was in him, and this life gives light to the world. A world as dark as ours is in need of the light of God, and it arrived one night in a manger. All of creation had been waiting since Eden for the dawning of this baby's birth.

And then the child grew and the word spread. He was different. So much like us, yet so different from us. We have both light and darkness threaded into our hearts. We can see both dawn and dusk in our souls, but he was light with no shadow, illumination with no night.

That first Christmas God sent a light so strong we would never have to be afraid of the dark again.

"Daddy, will you smile at me?" the children of Israel asked.

"Yeah," said God, climbing into a manger.

touching the unseen

whisper past me,
leave me in the wake of your words,
stunned into silence, enlightened by
the wonder of your presence.

    the night of your birth is a question
    wrapped in a question to me.
    unwrap them one by one
    and reveal yourself to my soul
    with the light that springs
    from your ever-dawning heart.

in a whisper of light you landed in a manger
i am living for the day you will land
in me.

conception.

i am a story hoping to unfold
as my future meets
my past

i am a tale waiting to be told
with the right words, now,
at last.

꙳

The Word became flesh and blood, and moved into the neighborhood.
> —*the apostle John describing the birth of his friend Jesus*
> *(John 1:14 Message)*

There's a Jewish saying: "God created man because he loves stories." I think that has a lot of truth to it. But not only does God love stories, he loves the people whose stories are being told moment by moment across the globe. And I'm amazed that the story of my choices, mistakes, regrets—the story of my life—actually matters to God.

I think what makes us unique isn't so much our height or shape or fingerprints or eye color but our histories, our stories. Day by day our lives are woven into a giant narrative, and every moment we become more and more the story of who we are. We *are* our stories. And we only connect with other people when we know their stories. The more intimate we are, the more our stories intertwine. That's one reason divorce is so painful—because it rips a single, deeply threaded story apart into two.

Sometimes I think about all the billions of stories swirling around each other on this planet, touching, deepening, unfurling, unraveling. And each one of those stories, each one of those people, mattered so much to the Author of Life that he left heaven and began the dreadful trek to the cross (see John 3:16). The original script called for unity and harmony, but our first parents chose to derail the story of humanity into a graveyard.

"Okay," said the Creator. "Then I'll tell a new story. One that includes a detour through an empty tomb." But to make that tale come true, he had to enter our story himself.

When Jesus was born, the Word of God became flesh, enmeshed in a story. The storyteller entered the tale. The author stepped onto the page. The poet whose very words had written the cosmos became part of the text of this world.

Like the harmony and the melody living together in the same song, Jesus was divinity and humanity living together in the same heart. He was the Word of God, God's story, in the flesh.

> i went looking for you.
>
> first, i searched through the tomes of church history, the volumes of philosophy, and the writings of the great and holy men . . . but you were not in the books.
>
> then i walked the hills and listened to the creek and learned the ways of the stars and the seasons . . . but you were not in the wilds.
>
> then i looked inside myself and my own knowings, to my will and my reason and my mind's discernment . . . but you were not in my heart.
>
> then i met a man who told me who i was and who whispered to my spirit the truths of my soul and told me stories that echoed with the longings of my heart. and you were in his stories.
>
> then i saw that you had been in the books and the forests all along. for at last you were in my heart.

✢

When Jesus came to earth he brought along the folktales of heaven. He didn't lecture like a professor but told fables like a bard, weaving tales of another world into the fabric of human lives.

He told stories because he knew humans are rarely interested in truth unless it's wrapped up in a story. He taught through stories, used stories to explain himself to his detractors, and helped people with eternal hungers get a foretaste of heaven through his parables. In fact, for a period of time, storytelling was the only way he taught: "Jesus spoke all these things to the crowd in parables; he did not say anything to them without using a parable" (Matthew 13:34 NIV).

Most of his stories were metaphors of heaven. He described the kingdom of heaven in terms of shepherds who would risk their lives for their sheep, women who can't find enough excuses to celebrate with their girlfriends, and fathers who party till dawn with their wayward sons.

In his stories, kingdom dwellers aren't just monks or mystics, priests or clerics, but jewelers, treasure hunters, bridesmaids, fishermen, farmers, business executives, outcasts, widows, prostitutes, and thieves.

And I love how irreverent Jesus is in his stories. He compared himself to a chicken, the coming of God's kingdom to a robber breaking into your house, God's message of hope to an uncorked bottle of wine, and prayer to a nagging neighbor hungry for a sandwich at midnight.

According to Jesus, we can learn about God's kingdom from eccentric landowners, dishonest managers, idiots who build condos on quicksand, demon possessed do-gooders, a warm loaf of bread, a field full of weeds, and a little kid tugging at your pants leg asking you to come outside and play. The kingdom of heaven unfurled from his lips in story after story after story.

you untangle the mysteries,
you whisper forth the parables,
you live within the fairy world
and light up the real world
with your tragic magic and your
heart full of blood.

☩

When Christianity becomes something other than entering into and living out the story of God, it becomes something other than Christianity. God's story isn't over; it's still being told today. Each one of us has the potential to become both a chapter of history and his story.

Yet with each story Jesus told, the religious leaders became more and more aware that this troublesome rabbi was using his parables to teach lessons they didn't like. When he finished one especially pointed tale, they'd had enough: "The Jewish leaders wanted to arrest him for using this illustration because they realized he was pointing at them—they were the wicked farmers in his story. But they were afraid to touch him because of the crowds. So they left him and went away" (Mark 12:12).

But they didn't stay away. The people Jesus had come to enlighten began to plot ways to silence heaven's storyteller forever.

☩

ah, sweet storyteller
what will it take to slay the dragon
and rescue your future bride?
    in your hands straw becomes gold,
    rags become linen,
    and thorns become roses—
    dew-covered, scarlet, and fragrant forever.
speak your tale into my heart
so that my life might finally make sense.

narration.

mystery

mystery of mysteries,
truth of all truths,
finder of the lost,

here i am.
unriddle me.

☩

Christ is God's ultimate miracle and wisdom all wrapped up in one.

*—Paul's description of the mysterious man who transformed his life
(1 Corinthians 1:24 Message)*

I used to think I knew Jesus because I knew about him. But knowing someone's resume and being someone's brother are two completely different things. I found that out after I met Jesus for myself.

If you can make sense of Jesus, explain him, define him, or make him sound reasonable, my guess is you've never actually met him. After all, his closest friends didn't understand him, the religious rulers thought he was possessed by demons, and his own family thought he'd gone insane. No one knew what to make of this man of mystery. I guess that's what happens when God dresses in skin, when heaven's wisdom speaks human words.

The greatest mystery of Christianity isn't that God loves us; nearly every religion would tell you that much. The greatest mystery is that God actually became one of us: "Without question, this is the great mystery of our faith: Christ appeared in the flesh and was shown to be righteous by the Spirit. He was seen by angels and was announced to the nations. He was believed on in the world and was taken up into heaven" (1 Timothy 3:16).

In Colossians 2:2–3 Paul calls Jesus, "the mystery of God . . . in whom are hidden all the treasures of wisdom and knowledge" (NIV).

Jesus is a holy conundrum. A living enigma. A mystery. He was born helpless and yet almighty, temporal and yet eternal, human and yet divine. He grew to become a carpenter who was wildly meek, quietly loud, furiously patient, humbly proud. He was the bringer of both peace and a sword, of both clarity and confusion, of both judgment and pardon.

> i don't name you, you name me.
> i don't understand you, you understand me.
> and the paradox of this love is that you uncover me
>   as you unveil yourself.
>
> the mystery of this discovery swallows all of who i am.
> that's the essence of faith.
> if i could understand faith it would cease to be faith.
>   i only know the mystery
>   because the mystery knows me.

⁜

Jesus was too normal-looking to arouse suspicion. He didn't stick out in a crowd. In fact, Judas had to point him out to the soldiers so they could identify him when they arrested him. He was that forgettable. And yet he's the most memorable and influential man in the history of the world.

He spoke in the riddles of a mystic, yet with the authority of a God. He was both humble and audacious, both soft-spoken and fiery, full of both sorrow and joy. No one has ever been meeker. No one has ever been bolder.

Jesus, the real Jesus, is earthshaking. He will both calm your soul and send a tidal wave of truth crashing through your spirit. As soon as you try to figure him out or wrap your mind around him, you'll get lost in the mystery of this man.

child of heaven,
    son of earth.
fragrance of light,
    strength of eternity.
former of worlds,
    shaper of souls.
storm of glory,
    love of God.
tamer of tempests,
    raiser of the dead.

offender of the religious,
    befriender of the outcast.
lion of conquest,
    lamb of sacrifice.
hero of the ages,
    talebearer of eternity.
king of all kings,
    servant of all servants.
calmer of consciences,
    disturber of the peace.

He is the mystic, majestic, mysterious Jesus. Holiness wrapped in humanity. He sneezed, coughed, yawned, burped, and got the hiccups, and yet he could walk on water, step through walls, and raise the dead.

When you try to prod at him, he prods at you. And when you finally meet him face-to-face, he'll shake your world—hardened criminals have been known to fall to their knees, shield their eyes, tremble, and weep at his feet. That's what happens when the veil is lifted and you finally glimpse his terrible, irresistible, glorious, soul-consuming love.

⁊·

Theology is the greatest threat to spiritual pilgrims when it becomes the game of defining God and gets in the way of letting God define you. I think the wonder tales—fantasies and fairy tales—lie closer to the heart of the Easter story because they acknowledge the reality of good and evil, the battle between right and wrong, the power of the supernatural, and the wonder of a world where dreams actually do come true.

If you try to divorce the mystery of Jesus from Christianity, you'll be left with just another religion, and a not very interesting one at that. Mystery lies at the heart of this story.

When Jesus calls us to believe, he calls us to step out on a limb, not to fall back into our comfort zone and rely on our own reasonable opinions. He calls us to a radical commitment, never to a practical religiosity.

And I think that's good, because it seems to me that people today are hungry for mystery again. Philosophy has given us questions; science has given us facts. But neither of those fill our souls. Jesus gives both truth hidden in mystery and mystery hidden in truth. In this way he can give both our heads and our hearts what we long for most.

The story of God becoming man is incomprehensible. Only fools would dare to believe it. And the idea that God loves us enough to die for us? Preposterous. I'm staggered at the thought of the world-whisperer speaking my name, of the almighty breaking into song at the thought of me or coming to earth to die for me. Yet that is the truth, that is the mystery of Jesus.

God didn't send us a doctrine to learn, or a religion to live, or a philosophy to debate. He sent us a brother to love and a madman to trust and a servant to serve and a mystery to embrace. Within the mystery of Jesus, all that is foolish teaches all that is wise, all that is weak conquers all that is strong, and death itself is swallowed up by life. Here truth and mystery stand side by side and immerse hungry souls in their sea.

To enter the story of Easter, you have to pass through the gate of mystery.

Through the person of Jesus.

touching the unseen

the text of my life is in need of editing.
enter between the lines,
pick up the pen of your love,
let your mystery engulf my heart,
    rewrite me.

reveal yourself to me
even if it means that
i must disappear
into you.

inversion.

new wine

for your first step into the divine sea you could have
turned water into either blood or wine.
since it was a party you chose wine.

the blood would come later.

This miraculous sign at Cana in Galilee was Jesus' first display of his
glory. And his disciples believed in him.

—*the apostle John, remembering the day Jesus kicked off his preaching
ministry by turning a truckload of water into vintage wine (John 2:11)*

He stood waiting, expectant, his hand outstretched. But I hesitated. After
all, I'd never danced with a rabbi before. Alon, my husband of twelve
hours, gave me a little nudge. "Go on, Rachel," he said.

"Yes," I said finally. "Okay."

"Thanks," said Jesus. He took my hand and led me onto the dance
floor. Everyone nodded and stepped to the side to let the young rabbi
dance with the bride.

"I love weddings," he whispered to me.

And we began to dance.

The night before, I thought I was going to go crazy. I peered out the window again and again and again, waiting, wondering. What could be taking so long?

I scanned the dark street again. Nothing. No torches. No lanterns. Nothing. Crickets jabbered at me from somewhere in the shadows outside my window. Other than that, the night was quiet.

My dad walked up behind me and put his hand on my shoulder. "He'll get here when he gets here. Stop worrying. Have something to eat."

"But what if I miss him? What if he's not coming?"

I heard my father sigh. And beneath his sigh I heard something else. Music? Or maybe it was the wind—

"C'mon, hav—"

"Shh, Dad! Listen!"

There it was again!

I scanned the street. Yes! Yes! There! A torch! And also a sound, a song rising in the night!

"They're coming!" I cried.

"'Bout time," grumbled my dad. "I was beginning to wonder."

I could barely contain myself. The music and laughter echoed through the town now. People were stepping outside their homes along the narrow street and clapping along to the rhythm of the drums, holding oil lamps to light the way for the wedding procession.

Dust rose into the air, curling around the laughing torches. The whole town was dancing to my door.

Then I saw my groom.

"Rachel!" he shouted, and stretched out his arms. I burst from the house, into the music and the warm swirl of his embrace. I caught the smell of myrrh on his cheek and leaned against the strong depth of his chest.

Around us everyone, everyone, was dancing.

My mother had spent all afternoon weaving golden thread into my hair. Now, as I took Alon's hand and danced with him toward our wedding, my hair fluttered behind me as if it were alive. As soon as we arrived at his house, my aunts and cousins would braid it with pearls handed down from a dozen generations. We weren't rich, but my father spent all he could to help me look like a princess. It was my night. My wedding. Everything was perfect.

When we finally arrived at his house, Alon paused at the door. "Rachel," he whispered. "Your father has said yes to our marriage, but I would rather have your approval than his. You know the tradition—once you step across the threshold of my home, we're married—"

"Yes. I know."

"I don't want you to come in unless that *yes* comes from your heart and not just your father's."

In our country only a man of men would offer his bride such a choice. Without hesitation I stepped forward.

And that's when the real party began.

Everything was a whirlwind of sounds and lights and laughter. The giggle of little girls twirling around in their prettiest dresses. The shouts of young men trying to outdo each other on the dance floor and at the wine cup. The quiet smiles of grandparents as they watched the wedding and the reception unfold.

And my husband, that dark curl of hair falling over his left eye, the feel of his beard against my cheek when we kissed, the strength of his hands around my waist.

Every moment was a girl's dream come true.

A young rabbi had come; my parents had invited him. At one point he stood and offered a blessing to our union and a prayer for our happiness. He was dancing a lot too. He seemed to really be enjoying himself.

⁂

But a few minutes after the blessing and the toast I noticed it. Something wasn't right. Just an undercurrent of confusion at first, whispered conversations between my mother and the mother of the rabbi. More whispers. Then nods.

There's a problem, I thought. *There's a problem at my wedding.*

Weddings are a big deal where I live. The party can go on for a week or more. Usually, it's at the groom's house. So Alon's family was hosting the party. Sometimes more people show up than you expect and you don't have enough food on hand. Or enough wine. And believe me, if there's one place you don't want to run out of wine, it's at a Jewish wedding.

Jesus's mother was whispering to him, then he was whispering to the stewards.

I watched from a distance. The waiters were acting strange. Stealthy. They went over to the water vats, and the next thing I knew they were handing out wine all around, laughing. I edged over to the vats and looked inside.

They were filled with wine. Hundreds of gallons of wine.

What?

It should have been water. I glanced at Jesus. He smiled at me, raising his cup.

Wine? But how?

I hurried over to tell Alon what was going on, but the caterer in charge of the banquet stepped between us, smiling broadly, swaying slightly. Apparently he'd been making sure the wine was suitable for human consumption.

"You!" he said, winking. "You sly dog, you!"

"What is it?" asked Alon.

"Everyone serves the best wine first—*hiccup*—and then when the guests have had a little—*hiccup*—too much to drink they pull out the cheap stuff. But not you! Oh no—*hiccup*—" He raised his cup high. "You saved the best for last!"

My husband looked curiously at the caterer and then at me. "I did?"

I nodded toward Jesus, who was finishing a dance with one of the bridesmaids. "Yes," I said. "You did."

"Ah yes, I did . . ." said Alon slowly. Still clueless.

The master of the banquet raised his cup again, took a long swig, and mumbled to himself, "I could use a refill, I think. Yup, saved the best for last."

He wandered off and Alon turned to me. "What's going on?"

"You're not gonna believe it—"

But before I could say another word, I felt a hand on my shoulder. I turned. Jesus.

"Congratulations, Rachel," he said, his eyes twinkling. He was a bit out of breath from the last dance.

"Thank you," I said, blushing.

"I love weddings."

"I can see."

Then he shook Alon's hand. "Now, you take good care of this bride of yours."

Alon nodded reverently. "I will, Rabbi."

Jesus leaned close. He spoke to Alon in an urgent whisper, but I heard every word. "Treat her like a queen, my friend. Love her as Yahweh loves Israel. Love her as Yahweh loves you."

Alon paused for a moment before answering. Now it was his chance to say *yes*. "I will, Rabbi. Yes. A queen."

Ah, Alon. My Alon! A man of men! I held his arm with both my hands. I never wanted to let him go.

Then Jesus smiled. "Good. Now, I'm sure you won't mind if I steal a dance from your bride, your queen?"

"Of course not."

Then the rabbi bowed to me and held out his hand.

Alon nudged me. "Go on, Rachel."

"Yes," I said finally. "Okay."

So I danced with Jesus as everyone else stood around singing and laughing and raising a toast to my marriage with glasses of this young rabbi's bubbly, sparkling, intoxicating miracle.

"Oh, I love weddings," he said.

"I can see," I said as he twirled me faster through the night.

꙳

Maybe it's just a coincidence that Jesus chose to kick off his public ministry by attending a wedding, but I doubt it. The more I learn about him, the fewer coincidences I see.

Here's the context: Jesus is thirty. He has spent the last decade or so working as a carpenter and has just recently shifted careers to become a rabbi. He was baptized, went on a retreat, prayed, fasted, withstood temptations from the devil, and recruited a handful of followers. You'd expect that kind of stuff from a religious leader. No surprise there. But then . . .

Does he found a church? Nope.

Apply for nonprofit status? Nope.

Go door-to-door peddling his worldview? Nope.

Instead he takes a bunch of his wine-guzzling drinking buddies to a weeklong wedding celebration, and when it looks like things are winding down, he turns 150 gallons of water into the best wine money can buy, just to keep the party going.

That's my kind of rabbi.

Jesus loved to party and was often disparaged by the religious fundamentalists because of it. One time he told them, "No one puts new wine into old wineskins. The new wine would burst the old skins, spilling the wine and ruining the skins. New wine must be put into new wineskins" (Luke 5:37–38). When God became man, he offered new wine to thirsty souls.

I'm thankful Jesus didn't come to start another religion. We have too many of those already. And I'm thankful Jesus didn't come to give us more laws, rules, regulations, or advice. Our world has enough of those too.

Instead he came to give us a fresh spiritual connection with God. As he told his followers, "Are you tired? Worn out? Burned out on religion? Come to me. Get away with me and you'll recover your life. I'll show you how to take a real rest. Walk with me and work with me—watch how I do it. Learn the unforced rhythms of grace" (Matthew 11:28–29 Message). Jesus came to pour new wine into our hearts and new hope into our lives.

Some people picture God as a doddering grandpappy in heaven. But in truth, he's more like an impassioned young lover swinging his bride across the dance floor. Jesus didn't arrive on earth to debate theology but to propose marriage. In a very real spiritual sense, God is courting us.

Christianity is wild. It's intimate. It's heartbreaking and soul-mending. It's the wings to rise above the everyday and the hope of a honeymoon with the God who has loved you forever.

The party has just begun, and the best is yet to come.

❧

dancing groom of the ages,
frolicking God awaiting his bride,
the wedding has just ended,
the party has just begun.

as your hopeful, blushing bride
i accept your hand and step with you
    into the heart of the music.

courtship.

i do not have to look at the sky
to know
where the sun is.
i can look at the ground,
to where the shadows fall,
and see where the sun
is not.

evidence.

✢

Some of the Pharisees said,
"This man Jesus is not from God, for he is working on the Sabbath."
Others said, "But how could an ordinary sinner do such miraculous
signs?" So there was a deep division of opinion among them. . . .
But despite all the miraculous signs he had done, most of the people
did not believe in him.

—*John, describing the deeply divided opinions concerning Jesus's identity*
(John 9:16; 12:37)

I think our world is full of mysteries and every moment holds the potential for the miraculous, yet too often we tune out the unexplainable or
relabel it to make it seem less baffling or less of a miracle. Take light, for
example. Depending on how you measure it, light seems to behave like
both particles and waves. Scientists keep changing their theories about

it. No one really knows what light is. After all these years, humans still don't understand something as common as daylight.

And then there's the magic of photosynthesis. Green plants spend their lives converting carbon dioxide (poison) into oxygen (life). Scientists can explain the process, but no one really knows how it all works. That's amazing to me.

Birds flawlessly navigate tens of thousands of miles; sea turtles head toward water when they hatch, even if it's out of sight. How? No one knows. I asked an educator at the world's most visited aquarium about the sea turtles, and she said, "They follow the moonlight."

"What if it's cloudy?" I said. She blinked and didn't really have an answer.

I thought maybe she'd say *instinct*. That's one of our favorite labels for the stuff we don't understand. It makes those things sound natural instead of inexplicable. That way we can talk like we understand our world even though we have no clue how it all works.

I don't understand love or birth or why I don't laugh when I tickle myself or how my eyes work with my brain to translate light waves (or particles) into images and colors in three dimensions. My skin is a mystery to me too. It keeps the rainwater out and the blood in. Yet even though I'm waterproof, I can sweat. It's nice too that the sweat can't get back in again. This isn't a major mystery to me, but at least it's a very convenient one.

Life itself is a mystery to me. How can someone be daydreaming or joking around with his buddies and enjoying a piece of leftover pizza one moment and then be a slab of cooling meat with a bullet hole in it the next? How can life just be over like that? I can't even comprehend it.

It's a mystery to me how no one can see, hear, touch, taste, feel, measure, weigh, or control my thoughts, and yet they're real. They exist, but no one can prove it. Scientists might be able to record electromagnetic impulses, but that's just evidence of brain activity; it's not the actual thoughts themselves. My thoughts are invisible and impossible to find. You can't cut my brain open and locate them. They're nowhere and yet right *here*. Every moment seven billion people are walking around thinking about sex or gorillas or cherry flavored yogurt, and with every thought we're immersed in a mystery that has baffled philosophers for thousands of years. And most of us aren't even aware of it.

I think gravity is a miracle we're still in the middle of. We don't know where it comes from or why it's there, so we call it a "law of science" instead of a miracle. I think it's a miracle God just hasn't turned off yet. Of course, it could just be planetary instinct.

> all around me,
> life is on fire, but it is not consumed.
> > buildings are burning
> > people are flickering
> > cars are bursting into flame
> and i marvel at the mystery of it all,
> with the smoke of life thick in my nostrils.
> then i hear a voice, deep within the passing of the day,
>
> > *remove your flip-flops!*
> > *for the sidewalk on which you stand is holy ground!*
>
> so i drop to my knees at the glory of the thunder,
> and i rip off my sandals and close my eyes
> and when i open them,
> the fire has gone out, but everything around me
> is holy.
> so *holy*!
> wrapped in the guise of the familiar.

＊

Jesus performed dozens of miracles. I love how his friend John put it: "Jesus' disciples saw him do many other miraculous signs besides the ones recorded in this book. But these are written so that you may believe that Jesus is the Messiah, the Son of God, and that by believing in him you will have life.... I suppose that if all the other things Jesus did were written down, the whole world could not contain the books" (John 20:30–31; 21:25).

That's a lot of miracles.

A few of the miracles Jesus's friends did write about include accounts of him walking across the surface of a lake during hurricane-force winds, setting victims free from demonic possession, healing incurable diseases from across town, feeding thousands of families with two tuna fish sandwiches, calming storms with a whisper, and making a coin appear in the mouth of a fish (*ta-da!*). He spoke and the blind were healed. The deaf could hear. The lame could walk. The lost were found. The dead were raised.

Or were they?

Should we accept these stories at face value or look for a logical explanation instead?

Scientists tell us that everything, including solid objects, is made up mostly of space. Maybe Jesus just knew how to rearrange the spaces between molecules so he could pass through doors, walk through crowds, step on water, remove diseases, and untangle eternity to awaken the dead. It was all just instinct. There, that explains it.

✝

An obscure passage in the book of Mark is as fascinating to me as all the accounts of Jesus's great miracles. Jesus was visiting his hometown, and the people there didn't believe in him. Mark writes, "And because of their unbelief, he couldn't do any mighty miracles among them except to place his hands on a few sick people and heal them. And he was amazed at their unbelief" (Mark 6:5–6). Mark doesn't say Jesus *wouldn't* do miracles; Mark says he *couldn't*.

I'm astonished that Mark mentions this, that he thought Jesus's *inability* to do miracles was newsworthy. You don't typically mention the fact that someone can't do mighty miracles: "Ricardo came over to my apartment this afternoon and he couldn't control the weather, walk across the swimming pool, or cure people of epilepsy! Can you believe it?" You'd never mention that—unless, of course, Ricardo typically *could* do those things.

I think Mark includes this incident because it was so remarkable, so unusual. Jesus was so mysteriously miraculous that the one time he couldn't do something amazing, Mark decided to write about it.

And what was it that caused this man who could control the weather and raise the dead to become powerless? The people's lack of faith.

Their unbelief was like kryptonite to Jesus.

Wild, huh?

The world of miracles is only visible and only available to those with faith. Jesus once said, "Anything is possible if a person believes" (Mark 9:23). The more we demand that God prove himself and make sense to us, the less he will. The door to the miraculous swings on faith.

in the seeking
comes the finding,
in the springtime
comes the bloom.
in the budding
comes the loving,
in the courtship comes the groom.

in the living
comes the dying,
in the doubting
comes the truth.
in the hoping
comes the dreaming,
in believing comes the proof.

⁒

Jesus didn't do miracles to get attention. In fact, most of the time when he did his miraculous signs, it was in spite of, rather than because of, the crowds. He never did miracles on demand. He wasn't into photo ops. Typically when a crowd of rubberneckers began to form, he would do his miracle quickly and then warn the bystanders not to tell anyone about it.

Jesus didn't want to become a sideshow attraction. That's not why he came. He just wanted to help people and have them believe in him. Here's a typical conversation between Jesus and the religious rulers:

Jesus told them, "This is what God wants you to do: Believe in the one he has sent."

They replied, "You must show us a miraculous sign if you want us to believe in you. What will you do for us?"

John 6:29–30

"Prove yourself," they said.

"Just believe me," he replied.

Believe. Believe. Just believe.

There's something supernatural about Jesus. We can't explain him. That's why people are either drawn to him or repelled by him. There's no neutral ground. Yes, the stories of his miracles are extraordinary, but we don't get to cut out the parts of his story that don't sound reasonable to us. We don't get to edit the story of God to fit our preferences. In exasperation Jesus once said, "Must I do miraculous signs and wonders before you people will believe in me?" (John 4:48).

Believe. Believe. Just believe.

The doorway to the miraculous swings open to all who dare to enter the mystery of faith.

⁂

touching the unseen

you stretch imaginations and souls.
you touch ears and eyes and tongues
and set them free.
you offer life to carcasses
dusty with the soil of everyday life.
    you are spirit.
    you are here.
do the first miracle of all in my life—
    help me to believe in you,
and set your mysterious strength loose
in my life.

power.

vagabonds

i lose myself in this
unveiling until there is
nothing left of me
but you.

꙳

As Jesus walked beside the Sea of Galilee, he saw Simon and his
   brother Andrew casting a net into the lake, for they were fishermen.
   "Come, follow me," Jesus said, "and I will make you fishers of men."
At once they left their nets and followed him.

   —*Jesus recruiting his first two disciples (Mark 1:16–18 NIV)*

Recently I read some stuff by the existential philosopher Søren Kierkegaard
that really shook me up. Here are a couple of excerpts from a collection
of his spiritual writings called *Provocations*:

In relationship to God one can not involve himself to a certain degree.
God is precisely the contradiction to all that is "to a certain degree."[1]

There is something frightful in the fact that the most dangerous thing
of all, playing at Christianity, is never included in the list of heresies
and schisms.[2]

The difference between an admirer and a follower still remains, no matter
where you are. The admirer never makes any true sacrifices. He always

plays it safe. Though in words, phrases, songs, he is inexhaustible about how highly he prizes Christ, he renounces nothing, gives up nothing, will not reconstruct his life, will not be what he admires, and will not let his life express what it is he supposedly admires.[3]

As I read and reread those blunt words, I had to ask myself, "Am I really a follower of Jesus, or am I just an admirer?"

I don't think there are too many followers of Jesus around anymore. There are plenty of churchgoing admirers, but most of us would rather not leave our nets behind and follow him. Instead we prefer dragging the nets onshore with us so we can have the best of both worlds. But of course that never works—you can't follow Jesus while you're dragging your old life along behind you. If you try to, you'll end up losing out on both. Every once in a while I get caught doing it—trying to pursue both what Jesus has to offer and what the world has to offer. But it's useless because they lie in opposite directions.

When Jesus called people to be his disciples, it always meant leaving something or someone behind.

"Follow me," he told his disciples.

"Follow me," he told the spiritually hungry.

"Follow me," he told the thieves, prostitutes, lawyers, and priests.

"Follow me," he whispers to us today. "Follow me."

Where? Toward what?

Toward the cross. The road Jesus walks leads all the way to the cross. It's there that old lives, old priorities, old selves have to be put to death. "Follow me," he says. It's both an invitation and a command. And he waits for only a moment to see what we will do.

Then he moves on to invite others.

Jesus is in the business of pursuing the lost but not of dragging them kicking and screaming into the kingdom. He never forced himself on anyone. He simply invites and lets us decide if we'll hang back or follow him. So Peter had to leave his boat, James and John left their father, Mary Magdalene left the ghosts of her past, Matthew left a lucrative career . . .

"Follow me," he said. And they did.

But not everyone did. Some people discovered how costly following Jesus really is and turned back. They started on the journey, but when Jesus didn't seem to fit into their neat, tidy little definition of a messiah, they left him. Sometimes they turned around because of spiritual questions, other times because of persecution or the lure of wealth or the worries of life or materialism or hedonism or realism or just plain boredom with the life Jesus offered.

At one point in his ministry, Jesus mentioned that unless the Father draws people, they'll never believe in him. Here's how his listeners responded: "At this point many of his disciples turned away and deserted him. Then Jesus turned to the Twelve and asked, 'Are you going to leave, too?' Simon Peter replied, 'Lord, to whom would we go? You alone have the words that give eternal life'" (John 6:66–68).

Jesus leaves the choice up to us: Who will we follow with our lives? What road will we walk? He invites; he doesn't coerce. He welcomes; he doesn't manipulate.

Jesus chose a rather unlikely group of fishermen, businesswomen, freedom fighters, and accountants to transform the world. Something in him spoke to them so deeply that they were ready to leave their old lives behind and walk in his shadow from then on. His words were sizzling sparks that set their souls on fire.

"Follow me," Jesus said.

And they did.

They became pilgrims walking toward an unseen land. Vagabonds. Nomads. Foreigners just passing through. Their home lay somewhere beyond the horizon. That's the disciple-life, the life of all who live by faith.

Once Jesus told his followers, "You can enter God's Kingdom only through the narrow gate. The highway to hell is broad, and its gate is wide for the many who choose the easy way. But the gateway to life is small, and the road is narrow, and only a few ever find it" (Matthew 7:13–14). After I became a believer, I wrote these words about the vagabond life:

> i see, in the shadow of my knowing,
> that i am not yet as real as love.
>
> yet in the light of this moment, i realize
> that i am at least on the right path.

✝

By the way, Jesus approached evangelism quite differently than most churches today. Too many twenty-first-century churches treat sharing Jesus's story like a marketing campaign. They try to make Christianity seem as appealing, plausible, relevant, and easy to digest as possible by emphasizing the benefits of belief. But Jesus almost never did that. Typically he emphasized the cost of following him, not the rewards. Here's what he told the crowds who had started following him: "Simply put, if you're not willing to take what is dearest to you, whether plans or people, and kiss it good-bye, you can't be my disciple" (Luke 14:33 Message).

There was no fine print in Jesus's call to discipleship. "This is what it's gonna cost you," he says. "Everything. Family relationships, possessions, dreams, comfort, time—you can't be my follower unless you give up everything. You have to leave your nets behind. So what do you say? Will you follow me, or just keep admiring me?"

It's rare to find people who are willing to give their all to God. Most of us are willing to give up *some* of our lives, *some* of our priorities, *some* of

our agendas, goals, desires, possessions, dreams, *some* of our hearts—but not all. "Let's not get carried away here," we say. "Let's be reasonable."

But there's nothing reasonable about denying yourself, following Jesus, and becoming a vagabond of heaven. It's the most unreasonable thing of all. And that's why only a few ever find the gateway to life.

Jesus never accepts half; he only accepts all. With him there's no wiggle room. We can't come to him with excuses, exemptions, or negotiations. We can never tell him, "Yes, but . . ." When one guy tried that, Jesus told him, "Anyone who puts a hand to the plow and then looks back is not fit for the Kingdom of God" (Luke 9:62).

Jesus isn't interested in admirers. He never was. And that's why his invitation was not "Admire me" but "Follow me." That's why he was so blunt with the crowds. Jesus didn't want a fan club. He wanted a spiritual revolution.

Early on in my life as a vagabond I discovered that following Jesus will cost me my pride, my ego, my rationalizations, my illusions, my demands, and my rights. That was a harsh lesson to learn. No longer do vagabonds have the right to hold a grudge, speak their mind, or get even. The only thing vagabonds have a right to do is to live and die for Jesus.

"Come, follow me," he said to Simon and Andrew. At once they left their nets and followed him.

Now it's our moment to decide what to do.

⁑

the path is narrow,
my heart is hard,
guide my feet.

break me, God,
for i will not bend.
and i'm not shaped as i should be
anymore.

submission.

shadows

> to a world used to darkness;
> to a people completely blind;
> light is not a savior . . .
> but a threat.

☦

The light from heaven came into the world, but they loved the darkness more than the light, for their actions were evil. They hate the light because they want to sin in the darkness. They stay away from the light for fear their sins will be exposed and they will be punished.

—*Jesus of Nazareth explaining the human condition to a Jewish supreme court judge (John 3:19–20)*

We live in an upside-down world.

All of us know we're going to die someday soon, but none of us live like it. We busily grasp at the mists as we step over the cliff. We hurt those closest to us and then spend our time worrying about what strangers think of us. We strive for positions of influence so we can control others, even though we fail daily at controlling ourselves.

Life is shadow and mirage. We spend our careers pursuing the two things we know corrupt people the most—power and money—all the while telling ourselves that they'll never corrupt us and that we're immune, even though we know we're not. We want popularity and fame and a good reputation, even though we know they're all vaporous and can be lost in a single day, or shattered by a single rumor.

We try to fill our eternal hungers with sex and self-esteem and good grades and designer shoes. We pack our lives with distractions in a desperate attempt to fill a hole in our lives we tell ourselves isn't there with things we know aren't important. We keep watching the commercials and we keep buying the stuff.

We wander farther and farther from home, convincing ourselves we're on the right track, until we finally arrive at the very state we've been fleeing from all along.

> i'm walking through the desert
> and there's no place for me to hide from the sun
> so i keep going, thinking that surely i'll eventually
> make it back to civilization and water
> and shade.
>
> but the sun doesn't rest and i grow more and more tired,
> too exhausted to scream at the sky and too weary to
> tell it to go to hell.
>
> i take one step after another, until a mirage appears.
> and even though i know it's all just vapors
> hovering above the sand,
> i'm comforted by the illusion
> once again.

All that matters in the end is the state of the soul, yet we worry instead about zits and hair color and abs and looking cool. Everything is upside down. We spend our lives planning for a tomorrow that never comes, dreaming of a someday that will never arrive, watching moments pass us by. And when you string enough wasted moments together, you get a wasted life.

We turn our backs to the flame and stare into the darkness because we think we already know what the fire looks like. But all too soon we forget about the fire as our vision is wrapped in shadows again. As God told the Israelites:

> Doom to you who call evil good
> and good evil,
> Who put darkness in place of light
> and light in place of darkness . . .
> Doom to you who think you're so smart,
> who hold such a high opinion of yourselves!
>
> Isaiah 5:20–21 Message

Darkness isn't too tough to find in our world. We don't have to look very far to find dark thoughts, dark deeds, dark words, dark and writhing shapes in our souls. The shadowy side of life is all too visible in the daily headlines, on the nightly news, or in the break room at work. Every one of us has secrets. All of us have a shadowy side.

Evil quietly slips through the doorway and into our souls when we leave the door open only a crack just to see what might happen. And when evil moves in, it moves in to stay.

※

Shadows stalked Jesus from the very beginning of his life.

Just after Jesus's birth, Israel's king found out about the prophetic child and sent executioners to kill him. But God warned Joseph, Mary's husband, in a dream, and he was able to escape to Egypt with his young wife and infant deity.

Later, when Jesus began to preach and heal and search for lost souls, the division between light and darkness became more stark. The more he ministered to the people, the more the shadows of anger and doubt and treachery began to deepen all around him.

As the light of his teachings spread, so did the shadows that were chasing it. Light and darkness. Yin and yang.

Jesus spent most of his ministry in the crosshairs of the darkness.

Then, toward the end, even his closest friends began to question him, to peel away at his resolve. The hypocritical religious leaders tried to trap him in blasphemy or perjury. People left him in droves when his teachings offended their sensibilities. His buddies began to plot and scheme ways to get a place of honor in his new kingdom.

The pathway before him became overgrown with thorns and overshadowed with death. And amidst the growing division surrounding him, one of his friends saw an opportunity for himself: "Judas Iscariot, one of the twelve disciples, went to the leading priests to arrange to betray Jesus to them. The leading priests were delighted when they heard why he had come, and they promised him a reward. So he began looking for the right time and place to betray Jesus" (Mark 14:10–11).

As Jesus headed toward Jerusalem and all the turmoil it contained, the shadows loomed larger and larger around him. But he didn't turn back. "As the time drew near for his return to heaven, Jesus resolutely set out for Jerusalem" (Luke 9:51).

His mind was made up. There was no turning back. His love for his bride and the dream of being with her forever drove him on.

Shadows pursued the light all the way to the cross.

✝

touching the unseen

shadows hunted you,
shadows loomed before you,
but you did not turn back.
i need some of your light to glow in my life
    and burn away the darkness
that dwells in the basement of my dreams.

i still have an echo of your image within me,
battling with this creeping stain upon my soul.
touch my heart with your fire
and cleanse me of the shadows
that i've been in love with for so long.

illumination.

venom

are the scars on your hands
shaped like nails,
or the piercing fangs
of a snake?

⸓

Jesus was in great anguish of spirit, and he exclaimed, "The truth is,
one of you will betray me!"

—Jesus's announcement to his followers on the last
night of his life (John 13:21)

I think the most successful lies are the ones that lie closest to the truth.
They're the hardest ones to spot because they look so much like truth
that they slip past us unnoticed. Then, choice by choice, we edge closer
and closer to the forbidden. Through little lies Satan makes rebellion
sound so reasonable and compromise seem like no big deal.

Judas Iscariot was one of the original disciples Jesus had chosen early in his preaching ministry. Judas was also highly trusted, having charge of the group's collective finances. But as Passover approached, "Satan entered into Judas Iscariot, who was one of the twelve disciples, and he went over to the leading priests and captains of the Temple guard to discuss the best way to betray Jesus to them" (Luke 22:3–4).

I wonder what lies Satan whispered to Judas, what truths he twisted in order to pry open the door to Judas's soul and convince him to betray his friend.

"Jesus needs your help, Judas. He needs someone to spark the revolt. It could be you. You could sit by his side in the new kingdom!"

"Jesus is a failure. He doesn't have what it takes. Why let this opportunity pass you by? Cut your losses. Make a few bucks and get out while you can."

"They won't be able to stop Jesus, so this way everyone wins. You get some extra silver, they get to arrest the prophet, and he gets to establish his kingdom. He'll thank you for it later. Trust me."

Why is it so easy to listen to the whisperings of a snake and so hard to hear the voice of the Lamb? Why are we drawn so naturally to illusion and so slow to pursue the truth? I think it's because ever since Adam and Eve's fatal choice, the jargon of temptation has been our natural tongue and the dialect of love has been a foreign language.

When I was a college sophomore struggling with a temptation I'd rather not mention right now, I wrote this poem:

dr. seuss meets mr. temptation

i think there's a thought that i thought was true,
though a naughty thought, i thought it grew,
when i thought the thought
and my thoughts were caught
by the naughty thought that i knew.

now, a naughty thought that starts to grow
may cause other naughty thoughts to flow.
and so i have fought
with the thought it has brought
other thoughts that i ought not to know.

the thought is so tempting but yet i dread,
the thought of that thought inside my head.
so, i think that i ought
to stop thinking that thought,
and start writing a poem
instead.

Writing the poem helped for a little while, but pretty soon I was
being tempted all over again to do something else. It's taken me a while,
but I've finally realized that no matter where I go or what I'm doing, I'll
never be immune from temptation. Never.

The evil one still hisses out his luring, juicy lies. His venom still in-
fects our choices, poisons our relationships, and distorts our priorities,
despite our best intentions and noblest goals. I think we don't notice
the glistening fangs because we don't want to. According to Jesus, our
souls prefer darkness to light (see John 3:19). So we step into the nest of
vipers time after time, even though we already know where it is and how

to avoid it, because there's nothing so alluring as the sweet whisperings of the forbidden.

> as you lick at your sweet dessert
> i wonder where else your
> tongue has been. how many others have
> tasted your kisses? how many other
> succulent treats have you eaten
> over the years, with your eyes closed
> and your heart swallowed in ecstasy?
> > i want to get up from the table and leave you alone,
> > leave you forever, but yet i stay
> > right here and watch your tongue
> > flick in and out . . . in and out . . .
> > as i feel your hand slide farther
> > up my leg beneath the table.
> fallen souls are such easy prey for snakes.

⸖

I don't suppose many people believe in the devil anymore, or at least if we do, we don't take him very seriously. Maybe we think he's symbolic of the evil in all of us, or a mythic representation of our greatest fears, or a literary device used to explain the inexplicable evil of our world. I don't know.

Whatever you may think of the devil, Jesus believed in him and took him quite seriously. Jesus always referred to Satan in personal terms rather than symbolic ones. Jesus called him "the evil one" (John 17:15), not "the evil idea." Once Jesus called him "the father of lies" (John 8:43–45), not "the symbolic representation of things that aren't true." Jesus viewed the devil as a real adversary in the real world.

Jesus warned his followers about listening to Satan, prayed for God to protect them from Satan, and told them to ask for their own protection as well. "Don't let us yield to temptation," he taught them to pray, "but deliver us from the evil one" (Matthew 6:13).

The ancient adversary of God was the one tempting Eve with the fruit, luring Cain into the field, weaving doubt into the minds of the Israelites, coaxing Jesus to prove himself in the wilderness, and now possessing Judas during the Passover feast. He slithered through all of history to strike at the heart of God.

Jesus once said, "This is war, and there is no neutral ground. If you're not on my side, you're the enemy; if you're not helping, you're making things worse" (Luke 11:23 Message). Now as Jesus entered Jerusalem and the Passover celebration drew near, Judas chose a side. This friend of Jesus chose the way of the snake.

✝·

<u>touching the unseen</u>

darkness swirls around me,
laughing wicked thoughts,
clawing at my feet.
it's so easy to slip
when i'm living this close
to the escarpment of hell.

o lord of life,
draw me closer to the light!
let love become the language
of my heart once again.

translation.

in the old testament,
moses and joshua took off their sandals
because they were standing on holy ground.

in the new testament,
you removed the sandals of your disciples
to clean their feet.

go figure.
who's standing in whose shoes now?

✢

He took a loaf of bread; and when he had thanked God for it, he broke
it in pieces and gave it to the disciples, saying, "This is my body,
given for you. Do this in remembrance of me."

—*Jesus's words at the Last Supper (Luke 22:19)*

I've always liked movies that have a twist at the end: *The Sixth Sense, The Others, The Game, The Spanish Prisoner, The Usual Suspects, Vanilla Sky,* movies like that. I love it when all of a sudden the tables are turned, everything flips around, and nothing is as it seems. I love it when a movie gives me whiplash.

That must have been a little bit how the disciples felt during that last Passover supper with Jesus.

All twelve disciples were there, and they knew something big was up. They'd arrived in Jerusalem to cheering crowds earlier that week, but instead of taking advantage of his popularity, Jesus burst into tears. Then he sent the crooked money changers skittering from the temple. And he'd spent the last few days talking about death and the end of the world. Morbid.

Now they're all meeting secretly in the upper room of a friend's house. As the Passover meal is about to begin, Jesus pulls out a towel and wash basin and cleans off their feet. That was the job of a servant, not a respected teacher. So that was unexpected. After that he gets really upset and tells them they'll all fall away and one of them will betray him. Of course, they can hardly believe this, but he assures them it's true. Then Jesus hands out the bread and wine of the Passover meal and starts talking about how these objects are really his own body and blood.

Whiplash.

⁜

For a while I went to a church where the pastor spent lots of time explaining the meaning and significance of the Lord's Supper to us. It was very important to him that we got it right—that we agreed with his interpretation of the meal.

You see, some Christians believe the bread and wine turn into Jesus's body and blood when you celebrate this meal. Others believe that the body and blood of Jesus are mystically present in, with, and under the bread and wine. Still others take this to be a memorial celebration in which the bread and wine symbolize Jesus's body and blood. This issue has created a lot of division and hard feelings among Christians. It's one reason there are so many different denominations out there.

After I became a believer, some of my Jewish friends invited me to a Passover meal, and only after that night, when I saw the context of

Jesus's words for myself, did I begin to understand what his bread and wine comments were really about.

As you remember, the Passover was a way of recalling the old covenant, when God's judgment passed over the people and they were saved because the blood of a lamb was marking their doors (see chapter 6: chains, and Exodus 12). Now, in the upper room, Jesus established a new covenant, a new agreement to save people through the shedding of his own blood: "After supper he took another cup of wine and said, 'This wine is the token of God's new covenant to save you—an agreement sealed with the blood I will pour out for you'" (Luke 22:20).

The old covenant (or testament) is completed; the new covenant (or testament) is here. It's because of this meal that the Bible has two parts, two testaments. The old covenant has run its course, and now God's new covenant is to save us through the poured-out blood of the Lamb of God, Jesus of Nazareth.

I think the key to fathoming Jesus's meaning lies in that little word *my*. When Jesus says, "This is my body" and "This is my blood," he's recasting the whole story. The disciples would never have associated the bread and wine with Jesus but rather with the sacrificial lamb. So when he says "my body" and "my blood," it's as if he's saying, "You always thought this meal was about remembering the Passover lamb and the deliverance of God. Well, guess what? That was just the first half of the movie. Now the tables are turned. From now on it's about remembering *me* and the *sacrifice* of God."

Whiplash.

Jesus is the Lamb of God, the one they'd been waiting for, the one centuries of sacrifices had been pointing toward. And now he was talking about being killed. Nothing was as it seemed. The deliverer of the ages was feeding these twelve guys God's new agreement, and they remained clueless. The entire Old Testament had been foreshadowing this night, and none of the disciples even realized it.

Blindness isn't a result of too little light—that's darkness. Blindness is when you're not able to see when light is all around you. These guys were blind.

> someone pointed out to me
> that a pebble and a diamond
> are alike to a blind man.
>
> maybe i've been fingering
> diamonds all this time,
> without ever realizing it.

The bread and wine were really diamonds of God's promise in disguise.

This meal was Jesus's way of integrating his life with all the Old Testament promises. As Jesus said during his famous Sermon on the Mount, "Don't suppose for a minute that I have come to demolish the Scriptures—either God's Law or the Prophets. I'm not here to demolish but to complete. I am going to put it all together, pull it all together in a vast panorama" (Matthew 5:17 Message). The ancient echoes were all about him.

Through his brokenness and death, hope would finally become tangible and real—as real as a warm loaf of bread or a cup of sparkling wine.

Different denominations will probably always wrestle with the exact meaning of the bread and the wine. But all of them agree that this meal is a way of remembering Christ's sacrifice, of receiving reassurance of his forgiveness, of proclaiming his death, and of expressing unity of faith. Paul explained it like this: "When we bless the cup at the Lord's Table, aren't we sharing in the benefits of the blood of Christ? And when we break the loaf of bread, aren't we sharing in the benefits of the body of Christ? And we all eat from one loaf, showing that we are one body" (1 Corinthians 10:16–17).

The blood of the lamb would be shed, the body of the lamb would be offered. And not just any lamb long ago in Egypt but the long-awaited Lamb of God himself now in Jerusalem. God's love, broken and bleeding. Their Savior would die so that they might finally live.

Whiplash.

The stunned disciples ate and drank and sang a hymn together, then headed out with Jesus into the night.

✢

touching the unseen

the sweet wine of your blood is on my lips,
the tender mystery of your body is on my tongue.

in the background of this meal i can hear
the desperate shrieks of the egyptians
and the gentle whisper of death passing over
        the doorframe of my soul.

your heart was broken on that cross,
and your blood has soaked deeply
into the wood of my days.

remembrance.

garden

tears and sweat and heartache
have always been
the most potent ingredients
of a vagabond's prayer.

And they came to an olive grove called Gethsemane, and Jesus said,
"Sit here while I go and pray." He took Peter, James, and John with
him, and he began to be filled with horror and deep distress. He told
them, "My soul is crushed with grief to the point of death. Stay here
and watch with me."

—*Mark's description of the prelude to Jesus's prayer in the*
Garden of Gethsemane (Mark 14:32–34)

After the Passover meal, after breaking the bread and sharing the wine
and ushering in God's new agreement sealed in blood, Jesus took his
friends to a quiet place to pray. His grief and horror were so deep he told
them his soul was crushed with sorrow to the point of death. Then he
asked three of his closest friends to stay alert and wait for him while he
went off by himself to pray.

He went on a little farther and fell face down on the ground, praying,
"My Father! If it is possible, let this cup of suffering be taken away from
me. Yet I want your will, not mine."

Matthew 26:39

He prayed more fervently, and he was in such agony of spirit that his sweat fell to the ground like great drops of blood.

Luke 22:44

This scene is so human it makes me uncomfortable. Jesus is so hurting and helpless and desperate, it makes me question things. It makes me wonder if maybe someone didn't get it wrong when they wrote this stuff down. Could it really be that Jesus wrestled that much with God? Was Jesus really praying in "agony of spirit"?

Apparently, yes.

I know that some Bible scholars have clever ways of looking at this text to make it seem more spiritual or reverent or holy than it appears. It's almost like they feel the need to rescue Jesus from our misconceptions. But the whole thing seems pretty clear to me. The eyewitnesses tell us Jesus was distressed, horrified, alone, crushed with grief, in agony, sweaty, and crumpled face-first to the ground. And based on Jesus's comments to Peter, this awful prayer lasted for more than an hour.

It sounds odd to say it, but Jesus wrestled with God that night in the Garden of Gethsemane. He wanted to walk another road instead of the one that led to the cross, but God told him no.

✢

in my heart is a wound
that is bleeding a prayer
one drop,
    one word at a time.

torn open by anguish
and drenched in despair,
one drop,
    one word at a time.

i didn't mean to cry
but my tears have escaped
one drop,
    one word at a time.

for this journey
has coated my soul with pain
one drop,
    one word at a time.

in my heart is a wound
that's as big as a prayer
one drop,
    one word at a time.

In Eden there wasn't much of a struggle. Adam and Eve gave in pretty quickly to temptation. They chose to go their own way rather than their Father's. But here, on this night, in this garden, Jesus chose the Father's way, the way of the cross.

Instead of his own pathway, he made the decision that he would submit to the Father's will no matter where it led him or what it meant.

I have a hard time grasping all of this. Didn't Jesus know that the empty tomb lay beyond the grave? A bunch of times he'd predicted he would rise from the dead, so he had to be expecting a happy ending. Why was he in so much anguish, then? Why such horror and deep distress?

I think it's because he was just as human as we are. To save us, Jesus had to suffer for us. And that meant going all the way, taking all the punishment that we had coming because of our rebellion. All of it.

He knew that meant more than just exquisite physical pain; it meant complete spiritual abandonment. And no pain from here to eternity is greater than the pain of knowing God has turned his back on you.

And yet he told God yes. Even if it meant suffering the ravages of hell, he would do it. No matter where it took him. No matter what it might mean. Jesus said yes to God.

☩

I think we all reach the question of the garden at some point in our lives. A moment comes when we have to decide: Will I go my way or God's? Will I follow my path or his? Will I choose the sensible, practical route of doubt, or is my faith big enough to say yes to God no matter where it leads or what it means? Jesus faced that choice in the Garden of Gethsemane. It wasn't easy. It was painfully, distressingly, achingly real. But he said yes to the Father.

And he didn't have to, he *chose* to: "Though he was God, he did not demand and cling to his rights as God. He made himself nothing; he took the humble position of a slave and appeared in human form. And in human form he obediently humbled himself even further by dying a criminal's death on a cross" (Philippians 2:6–8).

Jesus said yes to the cross. Christ didn't just suffer for us. It's more than that. He did it voluntarily. He had the power not to suffer, but he chose the path of suffering. That's the kicker. He chose the pathway of pain—he didn't simply endure it, he chose it. Why? Love: "We know what real love is because Christ gave up his life for us" (1 John 3:16).

Jesus had before him two paths—one of comfort and one of pain. He could run from God or say yes to suffering. His love caused him to choose the second of the two. Hebrews 12:2 says, "He was willing to die a shameful death on the cross because of the joy he knew would be his afterward." What joy? The joy of reunion. Of meeting his bride at the altar. Of welcoming us home to heaven.

Because of his love for you, Jesus said yes to the cross.

Then, when his prayer was over, he returned to his friends only to find them fast asleep. He woke them and pointed at the shadows. "Still sleeping? Still resting? Look, the time has come. I, the Son of Man, am betrayed into the hands of sinners. Up, let's be going. See, my betrayer is here!" (Matthew 26:45–46).

The wrestling match is over, the disciples are awake, and the betrayer has arrived.

✴

Jesus,
you wrestled with God
that night in the garden.
so you know how it feels.
i wrestle with him too
more than i'd care to admit.

help me to say those words with you:
    "your will, not mine be done."
    i need to say them now, pray them now.
unwrap my hesitation
until it becomes a welcome mat
on which you can wipe your feet
when you finally come home
to stay.

surrender.

i have kissed you so many times,
in betrayal and denial
that my lips hurt.

what kind of love is this
that still dares to call me
friend?

✝

Judas came straight to Jesus. "Greetings, Teacher!" he exclaimed and
gave him the kiss.

—*Matthew's eyewitness account of Judas betraying Jesus*
(Matthew 26:49)

Sometimes when I read about what Jesus said or didn't say, did or didn't
do, I remind myself that everything in his life was motivated solely by
love. Everything he did was totally in sync with the Spirit and in step with
the Father. That means that in every situation, the way Jesus responded
was the most loving way anyone could ever respond.

When I look at things this way, I often discover that love looks different than I expect it to.

For example, when a wealthy young man decided not to follow Jesus
because it would have meant leaving his wealth behind, Jesus let him go.
I probably would have handed the guy a tract or something. But Jesus
didn't, because he knew what real love looks like. This man wasn't ready
yet for the disciple life, so Jesus let him walk away (see Mark 10:21–22).

And when Jesus called the religious leaders hypocrites, blind guides, fools, show-offs, posers, sons of hell, and snakes who are filthy, greedy, self-indulgent, and bound for hell (see Matthew 23), those were the most loving things anyone could have possibly told them at the time. Being politically correct was not one of Jesus's strong suits. Loving people enough to tell them what they needed to hear was.

When Judas kissed Jesus, here's how Jesus responded: "Jesus said, 'My friend, go ahead and do what you have come for.' Then the others grabbed Jesus and arrested him" (Matthew 26:50). Jesus's words weren't soaked in sarcasm but in love. When he called Judas *friend*, I think he was saying the most loving thing in the world.

I've tried to picture that night in the Garden of Gethsemane. I've tried to hear the night sounds in the shadows and see the mists floating ghostlike through the trees. Over there is Jesus, a man scorched by prayer. Here are his friends fast asleep. Snaking toward us through the darkness is a torch-bearing crowd. Swords and spears glint in the moonlight.

I've tried to see the look in the eyes of those who've come to arrest Jesus. I think some of them are angry, but I'll bet most of them are scared because they've heard about Jesus. They don't want to fight a man who has the power to control hurricanes, knows the words to raise the dead, and has the courage to single-handedly clear the temple courtyard with a homemade whip.

They approach the olive grove where Jesus is talking to his friends. Then, a moment later, Judas strides toward Jesus, leans over, and kisses him on the cheek.

And then Jesus looks Judas in the eye and calls him *friend*. Jesus even asks him, "How can you betray me with a kiss? Of all the ways, Judas, how could you do it with a kiss?"

This was the most intimate of betrayals.

i have played the chameleon.
i have changed colors as i sit on this leafy fern and blend in so easily
    with the deep, ancient greens all around me. and i have fit in with
    the sandy, dun-colored soil and the patchy gray of the rotting tree.

every time i move around i watch my skin change color.
sometimes i try to be two colors at once or i forget what color i'm sup-
    posed to be
right now.

when that happens and someone notices she shouts, "look! what is
    that guy?! a lizard or a chameleon? he doesn't even fit in!"

"i'm a chameleon," i say, and quickly change my color so i look just like
    them.
once again.

☩

Jesus didn't use the word *friend* very often. I know. I looked it up. A
few times, in a general sense, he referred to his followers as his friends.
The only other people he called his friends were (1) a paralyzed man
whom he healed, (2) his buddy Lazarus whom he awakened from the
dead, and, according to some translations, (3) a guy who wanted him
to arbitrate his father's estate.

Judas was the only disciple we know of whom Jesus individually, spe-
cifically called his friend.

What kind of a man looks into the eyes of the one who is betraying
him, who is unjustly handing him over to die, and still calls him *friend*?
What kind of man does that?

A man of uncompromising, unfailing, indecipherable love.

Jesus the Nazarene.

For a while I used to wonder why Jesus didn't cast Satan out of Judas. After all, he'd sent demons out of people before. He could have saved Judas, right? Set him free from the devil? Why didn't he? I thought I finally had a question that cornered God.

But then I remembered that everything Jesus did was guided by perfect love. Judas had chosen his own path and priorities, just like that rich young man whom Jesus let walk away. Judas didn't want to be saved. Jesus had to let him go because Judas wasn't ready to be a follower.

Love has to let the beloved choose. Judas had made his choice. Jesus had to let Judas walk away because he wasn't ready to embrace the kingdom life. He'd never been ready. The lover gives the beloved a chance to say yes before stepping over the threshold. For three years Judas had said no.

In fact, earlier that night Jesus had told his disciples that it would not bode well for his betrayer: "Here at this table, sitting among us as a friend, is the man who will betray me. For I, the Son of Man, must die since it is part of God's plan. But how terrible it will be for my betrayer!" (Luke 22:21–22). Judas even ignored this warning and went ahead with his plan.

Judas's life had been an open invitation to Satan for a long time. Finally, the tempter just came in and shut the door behind him.

✢

After the soldiers arrested Jesus in the Garden of Gethsemane and all his disciples ran off into the night, the soldiers tied him up and led him to the high priest's home. "Inside, the leading priests and the entire high council were trying to find witnesses who would lie about Jesus, so they could put him to death" (Matthew 26:59).

Jesus was put on trial, but the verdict had already been decided: guilty. Even though the governor couldn't find anything wrong with Jesus, the religious establishment persuaded him to give Jesus a death sentence. And he did.

And only after the deed was done did Judas begin to realize who Jesus really was.

> When Judas, who had betrayed him, realized that Jesus had been condemned to die, he was filled with remorse. So he took the thirty pieces of silver back to the leading priests and other leaders. "I have sinned," he declared, "for I have betrayed an innocent man."
>
> "What do we care?" they retorted. "That's your problem."
>
> Matthew 27:3–4

When the priests refused to accept his change of heart, Judas spiraled into despair. He forgot who his truest friend was, and instead of turning to God for help or forgiveness, he chose to take his own life.

I know some people wonder if maybe Judas went to heaven because he felt guilty after his betrayal. But guilt doesn't save anyone. Faith does. And we have no evidence Judas had faith in Jesus. Gripped with guilt, Judas committed suicide even as Jesus was being led away to die for Judas's sins.

But couldn't Jesus have done anything more to help his friend?

Jesus was already doing everything he could. For three years Jesus had treated Judas in the most loving manner possible, offering him the kingdom of heaven repeatedly. But Judas walked away.

After the trials and beatings, Jesus was condemned to death: "When they were finally tired of mocking him, they took off the purple robe and put his own clothes on him again. Then they led him away to be crucified" (Mark 15:20).

If only Judas would have stayed around to see the rest of the story unfold, he might have seen his friend once again.

☧

touching the unseen

judas betrayed you for thirty pieces of silver.
forgive me for all the times i've done it
   for free.

yet you've chosen to call me friend.
help me to live like it.
i'm both captured and set free by
the mystery of your love.

enigma.

wounded

the greatest scars
are not found in wounded hearts,
but in overlooked ones.

there is no greater pain
than the ice of loneliness.

‡

From prison and trial they led him away to his death. But who among
the people realized that he was dying for their sins—that he was suffering their punishment?

—*Isaiah's prophecy about the death of Jesus Christ,
written nearly 700 years before his birth (Isaiah 53:8)*

I have a memory about Easter from the fog of my childhood. I don't
know if it's a real memory or not. Maybe it's a dream. Here it is: I'm at
a park pavilion on a rainy spring day. I'm watching the raindrops fall.
My parents are there.

Nearby, a hefty black woman is singing. Everything is in slow motion.
She closes her eyes and moves with the music, singing with her whole
body. In between the raindrops I hear her words enveloping the park.
She's singing an old spiritual song:

Were you there when they crucified my Lord?
Were you there when they crucified my Lord?

Oh, oh, oh . . . sometimes it causes me
To tremble . . . tremble . . . tremble . . .
Were you there when they crucified my Lord?

She really cuts loose on the "Oh, oh, oh" part, and when she says the word *tremble*, I do. A chill grabs hold of me and a shiver snakes down my spine.

In my memory, I want to either close my ears to shut out her song or open them wide enough to take her all the way into my heart; I'm not sure which. Either way, she goes through the whole song, and I'm about to cry, and it all feels like a dream, and the rain won't stop falling on the moist, green ground.

⸸

All the themes of the ancient story begin to merge now: creation, shadows, thorns, longing, blood, mystery, silence, venom, darkness. All the threads begin to weave together, all the notes form a single chord.

And the pattern that they weave and the chord that they play is this: pain.

Matthew remembers it clearly: "They made a crown of long, sharp thorns and put it on his head, and they placed a stick in his right hand as a scepter. Then they knelt before him in mockery, yelling, 'Hail! King of the Jews!' And they spit on him and grabbed the stick and beat him on the head with it" (Matthew 27:29–30).

His body is being beaten. His blood is being spilled. His heart is being broken.

For me.

And it causes me to tremble.

⸸

When I was a baby I was badly burned and almost died when a vat of boiling grease tipped off a countertop and splattered on top of me. I still have scars across my neck, chest, and left arm. As a kid, whenever I heard about hell, I'd picture those scars and imagine getting burned with hot grease over and over again but never dying. The scars would get deeper and thicker, but the pain would never go away.

I'm not sure anymore that's what hell is really like. While I'm sure the suffering has a physical aspect to it, when Jesus talked about hell, he described a torment that was both physical and emotional. That's because the deepest wounds, the gravest scars, don't appear on skin but in souls. In hell the tracks of isolation, despair, and hopelessness play over and over again forever, while heaven remains just out of reach. Those who refuse to enter God's story on his terms will regret it for an eternity.

I don't think anyone dies expecting to go to hell. I think most people die expecting to go to heaven or at least hoping God will grade on the curve and promote them even if they didn't quite finish at the top of the class.

> we frantically dance
> all around our demise.
> as we put on a mask
> and we wear our disguise.
> we blink and we wink,
> then we close both our eyes
> and we think we've escaped,
> but when death has her way,
> we awaken—
>
> and scream in surprise.

❧

In the Garden of Gethsemane, Jesus knew he would be experiencing the worst punishment hell had to offer. That's why his agony was so real and his grief was so deep.

Jesus had begged God for another way to rescue his bride, but the all-knowing God could think of no Plan B. If there had been any other way, he wouldn't have let his Son die. God isn't sadistic or vindictive. He is love itself.

So, in the tragic and glorious logic of love, God knew of no other way than this to both punish sins and to forgive them. Justice and mercy met on the cross.

I don't think the deepest scars, the greatest pains Jesus felt that day were from the barbed whips flaying his back, or the nails biting through his skin, or the thorns slicing into his scalp, or the thirst clutching at his throat. I think the greatest wound of all was this: he felt the pain of a soul abandoned by God. What deeper pain is there than that? Jesus felt the flames of hell lick at his spirit.

For you.

That was the final thorn.

The serpent coiled and struck, and the venom of our choices ran deeply through the soul of Jesus. Our vanity and selfishness and pride and misplaced priorities sent Jesus to die and to suffer the very essence of hell while his body hung pinned to the wooden beams.

To really understand Easter, I think we need to hear the barbed tails of the whip sail through the air. I think we need to picture Jesus's blood-stained tears soaking into the sand. But more than anything, I think we need to feel the rising terror of this moment. Jesus has been abandoned by the Father because we followed in the steps of Eve.

Don't turn away. Hear the painful cries of this man now, or you won't hear his invitation later. You can't accept his love until you realize his sacrifice.

Each step he took, he was taking for you. Each splinter stinging through his skin from the rugged cross on his shredded back, he took for you. Each wound he felt crying out in his soul, he accepted for you.

Each thorn had a name on it.

Yours.

He knows of no other way to save his beloved than this—to experience hell in her place, dying at her hands. At my hands.

And it causes me to tremble.

⸭

touching the unseen

i was there—
    in your heart
    on your mind
    within your love.
i was there when they crucified my lord.

shivers.

skull hill

when death fingered your throat,
hoping for a final victory.
it didn't realize that it was
actually strangling
itself.

☦

They took Jesus and led him away. Carrying the cross by himself, Jesus
went to the place called Skull Hill (in Hebrew, *Golgotha*).
There they crucified him.

—description of the place on the outskirts of Jerusalem where Jesus died
(John 19:16–18)

Why, Rabboni? Why?

The beams of the cross lie heavy across his shoulders. I watch as
he struggles toward the hill they call Golgotha. Skull Hill. The hill of
death.

How could this happen? Why do you let them do this to you?

All of his miracles flash through my mind—healings, turning water
into wine, telling demons what to do—I know all about that, about the
demons part.

Not so long ago I heard voices in my head, in my soul. They told me
to do unspeakable things. And I did them. I did them all. Everyone in
my hometown of Magdala was afraid of me. But Jesus, with his laughing
eyes and soft words, set me free.

Then he spoke my name: "Mary. Come, follow me."

And once I was free, I followed him. Where else could I go?

But now . . . Now . . .

Why doesn't he stop this? Where is all that power now?

I really thought he would be the one. We all did.

I can barely recognize him; welts and bruises hide his eyes, shredded flesh hangs from his back. He doesn't look at all like a mighty deliverer, like the promised Messiah. He looks like a broken man.

Isn't there anything I can do for you, Rabboni? Anything?

No. There's nothing I can do. Nothing anyone can do. And there's nothing he can do for me. Not anymore.

As we leave the city, the crowd swells around me, each face twisted in anger. The same voices that chanted his greatness a few days ago are screaming now for him to die. I don't understand it. Any of it. My ears are full of their poisonous words. Everything is happening too quickly. Dust from the shuffling feet of the crowd is choking me.

As I watch him stagger up the hill, tears begin to cloud my eyes. They've given his cross to another man now to drag the rest of the way up Golgotha. But that's only cruelty dressed up like compassion—this way Jesus will survive long enough to be tortured to death on the hill. Everything is spinning and ending. Everything is wrong.

"Why?" The word drops from my lips like a dead kiss. I had loved him, or do love him, more than I've ever loved anyone. I loved the calm ease that surrounded him, and the touch of his hand on my arm, and the deep glorious ring of his laughter. I loved his stories of heaven, and his riddles about God, and his mischievous grin.

At one time I'd dreamed of marrying him. He knew that, of course. And more than once I'd seen the flash of love in his eyes. Sometimes he spoke of the day he would marry, or of the dream of seeing his bride dressed in white. Whenever he did, my heart would race. But he didn't mean me. It wasn't meant to be.

Nothing was meant to be.

I'd thought he was the one, and now I don't know what to think.

The soldiers have him on the ground now. They're positioning the nails against his wrists. I shudder. I close my eyes. I can't help it.

"No," I whisper. I want to scream, but only a whimper escapes my lips. "No, God . . . please, not like this . . ."

And in the darkness beneath my eyelids, I hear the hammer blows echo across the hill and through my heart. And I know I'll always hear them, every time I close my eyes. Forever.

I shudder and try to look up, but I can't. I fall to the ground and whisper the words over and over again. "No, God . . . please, no . . ."

But it does no good. Yahweh is ignoring me.

Even with my eyes closed, I can feel the day grow darker all around me.

⁊·

God's love is so inexplicable and unfettered and extravagant that it's a mystery to me. Love is dying for his beloved there on Skull Hill.

The wounds on his back are crying out. The lashes are cutting deeply through his soul. There's agony on his face, but it's a deeper agony than whips or thorns or nails can bring. It's the growing agony of loneliness. For this man is being despised and forsaken by his friends, by his bride, by his God.

Six hundred and eighty years before Jesus was born, Isaiah prophesied this would happen:

He was despised and rejected—a man of sorrows, acquainted with bitterest grief. We turned our backs on him and looked the other way when he went by. He was despised, and we did not care.

Yet it was our weaknesses he carried; it was our sorrows that weighed him down. And we thought his troubles were a punishment from God for his own sins! But he was wounded and crushed for our sins. He was beaten that we might have peace.

Isaiah 53:3–5

But how could his wounds heal us? How could his beatings bring us peace?

When I was a kid my pastor explained that God's forgiveness (he called it *justification*) was like a courtroom decision—God declaring us not guilty as he allowed his Son to be tortured to death in our place. I think I understand where that pastor was coming from, but the analogy never really resonated with me. Love isn't forensic and sterile; it's sacrificial. Grace isn't a decree; it's a gift.

In Hans Christian Andersen's original tale of "The Little Mermaid" (not the Disney version), a beautiful young mermaid has fallen in love with a human prince. The mermaid is a glorious singer beneath the sea, but she gives up her voice to be able to become human and love the prince. The deal is, if she can woo him, then she can remain human and receive an eternal soul. But if he marries another woman, the little mermaid will turn into sea foam, the fate of all mermaids.

Well, despite all her devotion to him, the prince's heart remains enamored with a different woman, a princess whom he believes rescued him from a shipwreck. However, the little mermaid was really the one who had saved him. She wants desperately to tell him that she was his savior and that she loves him, but she has no voice above the sea, no words he can hear.

In the end, all three are sailing back to the prince's palace for his wedding to the other woman. The little mermaid is about to turn back into sea foam when her sisters swim to the water's surface and offer her a knife and a choice: if she will take the prince's life, she need not give up her own. The magic can be reversed; she can become a mermaid again if only she will kill the prince. One of them must die before daybreak.

Everyone else is asleep on the boat. Silently the little mermaid approaches the prince and finds him in the arms of the other woman. As Hans Christian Andersen writes,

> The knife trembled in the hand of the little mermaid: then she flung it far away from her into the waves; the water turned red where it fell, and the drops that spurted up looked like blood. She cast one more lingering, half-fainting glance at the prince, and then threw herself from the ship into the sea, and thought her body was dissolving into foam. The sun rose above the waves, and his warm rays fell on the cold foam of the little mermaid.[1]

The prince knew nothing of her sacrifice, nothing of her love. He didn't know she had rescued him, given up her beautiful voice to become like him, and then exchanged her life for his. All this went on while he pursued another woman. She sacrificed all for her prince because she loved him, yet he never returned her love.

When the gospel is told like that, I can understand it.

God's love didn't happen in a courtroom but on a cross where Jesus threw himself from the ship and into the sea. The story I see woven all throughout Scripture is a tale of passion and sacrifice—not a deal brokered between a lawyer and a judge. It was a gift given from a lover to his beloved: in one final act of sacrificial love, he offers his life so that she might live.

We have a God who would let himself be nailed to a cross for his beloved. And there he would dare to die for her. For us.

Hold onto this moment. See him hanging there, between heaven and earth. Between God and humanity. See him dying there on Skull Hill. Don't turn away. Easter will never make sense without this moment.

⁜

touching the unseen

you know.
somehow, you know.
i can see it on the fringes of this story.
i can sense it being carried along
on the fragrance of your tale.

you know the ache in the back of my throat.
and the tears on the edge of my eyes.
   you know the state of my heart.

you threw the knife away
and slipped into the sea.
your cold foam washes over my soul
as i sleep beside my other lovers.
   what will i do about your love?

sacrifice.

darkness

darkness has been
waiting for this moment
since the beginning of time.

now, instead of nibbling
away at its meal,
it has swallowed the
light of the world whole—
in one great gulp.

⁂

At noon, darkness fell across the whole land until three o'clock. At
about three o'clock, Jesus called out with a loud voice, "*Eli, Eli, lema
sabachthani?*" which means, "My God, my God, why have you forsaken me?"

*—the dying words of Jesus of Nazareth as he hung on the cross
(Matthew 27:45–46)*

Jesus died.

I know this isn't how a story is supposed to go. The savior is supposed
to save. The hero is supposed to win. The good guy is supposed to come
out ahead. We know that because we know how stories are supposed
to end. So we assume Jesus didn't really die—maybe he's in a coma or
something, maybe his friends will storm the hill and rescue him at the
last minute, or maybe he'll escape just in the nick of time by using his

superhero powers or his utility belt or his multifunction Swiss Army knife. We know he didn't really die. Not really.

But we are wrong.

He did die. Jesus had no last-second escape. He died for real: "Jesus shouted, 'Father, I entrust my spirit into your hands!' And with those words he breathed his last" (Luke 23:46). Jesus died and darkness covered the sky. A soldier even confirmed his death by sliding the blade of a spear up between his ribs, carving a wound big enough to put your hand into.

In the end, even those watching him die could tell there was something extraordinary about this man. "When the captain of the Roman soldiers handling the executions saw what had happened, he praised God and said, 'Surely this man was innocent.' And when the crowd that came to see the crucifixion saw all that had happened, they went home in deep sorrow" (Luke 23:47–48).

That day on Skull Hill, the light of the world went out.

⳨

Over the years I've become more and more wary of people who try to make Christianity sound reasonable. God said his message would sound foolish rather than sensible, that it would be offensive rather than politically correct. The reality of the cross and the naked corpse of God is highly offensive. Until it offends us, we will never believe.

It's politically correct to say that God is love, but not to say that God showed his love by dying for us. That's offensive. We want an impersonal and impotent God who never actually shows love, just talks about it. Maybe we think he should just join our circle, sing the Barney song with us, and tell us all how special we are. That's how little we understand love.

Love sacrifices for the beloved. In this case, God gave his life for us. Jesus chose to offer his life in order to rescue us, his bride.

God's love is mysterious. Christianity will never make sense to your head. It's not meant to. But it will make sense to your heart—if you leave yourself open to the mystery of his love.

Our culture seems to think that the open-minded are those who remain indecisive about God and that religious people are close-minded. But in reality it's just the opposite. Here's what Paul wrote about people who have rejected God's story: "Their closed minds are full of darkness; they are far away from the life of God because they have shut their minds and hardened their hearts against him" (Ephesians 4:18).

Those who believe have opened their minds to the mystery. Those with closed minds have not. If we're ever going to accept the mystery of Jesus, we have to open our minds enough to accept this expression of his love: he died to set us free.

> When we were utterly helpless, Christ came at just the right time and died for us sinners. Now, no one is likely to die for a good person, though someone might be willing to die for a person who is especially good. But God showed his great love for us by sending Christ to die for us while we were still sinners.
>
> Romans 5:6–8

Christianity is not content to say that Jesus was simply a good man, a wise moral teacher, a political revolutionary, or a martyred prophet. He was more. He was (and is) God himself. And so, when Jesus died, God himself died.

Christians believe that God exists in a mystical and powerful union of three personal entities in one unified deity—the Father who loves us, the Spirit who seeks us, and the Son who saves us. There is only one

God, not three. Jesus is the one true God. The Father is the one true God. The Spirit is the one true God. Yet there is only one God. It's a riddle. It's a mystery. It's Christianity.

So when the Son died, God himself died.

Nietzsche was partly right—not that "God is dead," but he *was*. God died on Skull Hill. And for three hours on a Friday, even the sun hid its face.

> winter devoured spring
> on a hill far away.
> death devoured life
> on that cold and chilling day.
> > the author of the universe,
> > the poet of the stars,
> > died upon a rugged wooden cross.

> pain conquered joy
> when the carpenter was killed.
> hope cracked in half
> on that crucifixion hill.
> > the savior we had waited for
> > the lord we'd hoped would reign.
> > died upon a rugged wooden cross.

> the groom did not complain
> as he suffered for his bride
> yet the people turned their backs
> on the day the prophet died.
> > the hope of all his followers,
> > the dreams of all mankind.
> > died upon a rugged wooden cross.

All the cosmos shook the day God died. Earthquakes, a solar eclipse, graves spitting out their dead. Our world was never designed to withstand the death of its maker. The earth and sky and sun and stars all shuddered and tried to close their eyes and look away. A chill ran down the spine of the universe.

What else would you expect at the death of the Creator? Hopelessness climbed up from the grave, up from the depths of hell, and took over the world the day Jesus died. Creation has come full circle. The darkness that had lived with God from the beginning of time swallowed up the sky.

Leave it to humans to snuff out the light of the world, to kill the man who had come to be their Savior. "Every day I was with you in the temple courts," said Jesus when the priests had come to arrest him, "and you did not lay a hand on me. But this is your hour—when darkness reigns" (Luke 22:53 NIV).

Darkness reigned that day. And Jesus died.

✦

touching the unseen

sunlight wrestles
with the rising night,
but it is tired.

hope is dying around me.
meek and worn, fading into
darkness
without a groan.
without a peep.

then the coffin of darkness closes
and i am inside it
when the light goes down, dead
into the grave.

crossroads.

scattered

some sheep aren't lost
they know exactly
where the shepherd is.
it's just that they're running
away from him.

⸙

"All of you will desert me," Jesus told them. "For the Scriptures say,
'God will strike the Shepherd, and the sheep of the flock will be
scattered.'"

—Jesus, predicting that his disciples would abandon him
(Matthew 26:31)

All his disciples deserted him and ran away.

—less than ten hours later, when his words came true (Mark 14:50)

What a place to be in.

Sometimes I try to imagine how those first vagabonds must have felt.
They'd staked their lives, their futures, their eternities on this man, this
indestructible and yet fragile Savior. And now he's dead, and so are all
their dreams. Their Savior has been slain.

Afterward Joseph of Arimathea, who had been a secret disciple of Jesus
(because he feared the Jewish leaders), asked Pilate for permission to

take Jesus' body down. When Pilate gave him permission, he came and took the body away.

Nicodemus, the man who had come to Jesus at night, also came, bringing about seventy-five pounds of embalming ointment made from myrrh and aloes. Together they wrapped Jesus' body in a long linen cloth with the spices, as is the Jewish custom of burial.

John 19:38–40

Where do you turn, what do you do when your Savior lies cold and dead at your feet? I guess you stick him in the grave and toss dirt over his body like any other dead guy. What else is there to do?

Take out the dead and get on with life.

Nothing makes sense. Nothing seems trustworthy and sure. Reality is splintering around you. The one who claimed to be "the resurrection and the life" (John 11:25) is dead. Could it be that all of his promises, all of his teachings, all of his kingdom-talk was nothing more than wishful thinking?

Is anything real? Is anything true anymore?

He's dead. That's true. That's real enough. There's his corpse right over there.

What name do you give to the realization that all your beliefs were a cosmic joke? That all you held as true is illusion? How do you grapple with the knowledge that your Savior couldn't even save himself? Is there a word in any language that can speak the color of that emotion?

I don't know of one. *Despair* doesn't do it. *Hopelessness* doesn't go far enough. Whatever that terrible word is, they felt it wrenching through their hearts, leaving great scars in its wake. They had doubted him, deserted him, denied that they knew him, and now at last they gave up on him.

A secret disciple and a midnight visitor took care of his body. But where were the disciples?

Scattered. Hopeless. Hiding.

In the aftermath of Jesus's death, one of his disciples said this: "He was a prophet, powerful in word and deed before God and all the people. The chief priests and our rulers handed him over to be sentenced to death, and they crucified him; but we had hoped that he was the one who was going to redeem Israel" (Luke 24:19–21 NIV).

See that? They "had hoped." Past tense.

They don't hope anymore. Their hope had been put to death on the cross.

The shepherd had been struck. And the sheep went into hiding.

※

On the night of Judas's betrayal, Jesus's friends had all let him down. First they fell asleep while he prayed in the garden. Then James and John, who'd begged to rule beside Jesus, bolted into the night. Peter, the man who'd vowed he would die with Jesus, was too frightened to admit that he even knew him. Mark was so scared he ran off naked: "There was a young man following along behind, clothed only in a linen nightshirt. When the mob tried to grab him, they tore off his clothes, but he escaped and ran away naked" (Mark 14:51–52).

You don't hear the part about Mark running off naked too much in churches anymore. But that's how scared they were, how scattered. The disciples run off, and we don't see them again until Easter morning when Mary Magdalene comes knocking at Peter and John's door with the news of a missing corpse.

Here the story of Easter really gets personal—here, in the aftermath of Jesus's death, with his followers hiding like lost sheep. Because when I look in the shadows beside them, I see myself: hiding from God like

Adam and Eve, or slipping off to the field like Cain, or running into the night like Mark.

Some people leave the theater at this point. When their Savior lets them down, when their hero falls, when their drug doesn't deaden enough of the pain, they check out of the game, with a bullet in the head or a handful of pills. It happens every day. Because sometimes when we stare at the abyss it doesn't just stare back; it invites us to come over and play. It whispers to us, drawing us closer and closer to the edge. *Jesus is dead. There's no hope left. What's the use?*

If we don't hear the rest of the story, if we don't stick around until Easter, we'll be left in the shadows with Judas. We'll be left fumbling for a way out, trapped in the center of a long, narrow scream.

> where is the breeze that brings hope in its wings?
> where is the fragrance of life to be found?
> only on the other side of the grave.
> only on the other side of easter.

Jesus is dead. All they had hoped for, all they had believed in, all they had dreamed of came crashing down. It's time to bury their God.

They don't realize yet that if any of his words, if any of his teachings are ever to make final sense, he had to die. They don't remember his words, "When we get to Jerusalem . . . the Son of Man will be betrayed to the leading priests and the teachers of religious law. They will sentence him to die and hand him over to the Romans. They will mock him, spit on him, beat him with their whips, and kill him, but after three days he will rise again" (Mark 10:33–34).

They don't see the big picture; all they see is a corpse. His words are betrayals to them now. Broken promises made by a deluded man.

The shepherd has been slain. The sheep have been scattered.
And the wolves have been set loose.

touching the unseen

my prayers are vacant paragraphs
floating toward the edge of the truth.
why did it have to happen like this?
why did you have to die?
    hope in you seemed so reasonable
    only a moment ago.
    now, it all seems so ludicrous.

slain shepherd,
don't stop looking for me
don't stop searching.
find me,
here i am—
    wherever here is.

lost.

o jesus, i've come to pay my last respects.
thank you.

but the only spice i have to offer is the salt in my tears.
that is enough.

†

The next evening, when the Sabbath ended, Mary Magdalene and
Salome and Mary the mother of James went out and purchased
burial spices to put on Jesus' body. Very early on Sunday morning,
just at sunrise, they came to the tomb.

—*Mark, recounting when the women went looking for Jesus's body*
(Mark 16:1–2)

The women are on their way to the tomb to pay their last respects, to
finish burying their friend. Dawn is about to break loose across the land,
and in this moment before daylight the women have come.

Yesterday was the day of rest, and they observed it, dutifully, obediently, somberly. Now they carry spices to place on his body as their final
act of kindness. These are the women who provided for him during his
life; now they want to do the same for him in his death. Because they
love him.

The disciples are still hiding, but these women aren't. They want to
honor their Rabboni, and in their culture this is how you care for the
dead, with burial spices.

Their steps are heavy, though. Their faces drawn. Their eyes blood-shot, tired, and dry. They've almost run out of tears—almost but not quite. Yesterday, the day of rest, was their day of tears. "Today," they tell themselves, "today is the day to finish the job of burying the Lord. Tomorrow there'll be time for tears again."

The Magi, the wise men, had brought Jesus myrrh at his birth. Now these distraught women bring him myrrh again just days after his death.

> how do you care for a dead God?
> how do you bury the almighty's corpse?
> what spices will ever be enough
> to honor a fallen deity and to quiet
>   the decay of eternity in his heart?
>
> how do you care for the dead
> when the fallen one is the author of life?
>
> no incantation seems strong enough
> anymore.

❧

Here come the women, emerging from the forest, wondering how to move the stone and open the tomb. They saw where he was buried. They know the place. They saw the size of the stone used to seal the entrance and wonder how they'll ever be able to roll it out of the way. But still, they've come. This is their friend, this is their duty. They'll find a way.

Dawn is about to break. Sunlight is chasing them, hurrying toward the horizon as they pad silently across the dewy ground. Daylight is about to crack through the shell of the sky.

Finally, in the moment before sunrise, they arrive at the tomb. The shadows behind them are long. Light blazes into their eyes. The sun pokes over the horizon. It is finally dawn.

And they stare at the tomb.

Already the stone has been rolled away.

Easter is here.

⚼

touching the unseen

a moment ago sorrow swallowed
all of my joy,
all of life was a broken melody.

but now . . .
   what is this new tune that i hear?
   who has rolled the stone away?
i shudder as yet another mystery
engulfs me
and the new-day sun laughs above me
in the clear, expectant sky.

bewildered.

dawn

some lights are only made brighter
by putting them out.

⁂

They found that the stone covering the entrance had been rolled aside.
So they went in, but they couldn't find the body of the Lord Jesus.

—*Luke's record of the women's unsuccessful search for Jesus's corpse*
(Luke 24:2–3)

It just wasn't there.

They'd put his body in the tomb on Friday, but now it's Sunday and
the corpse is gone. Naturally, they thought someone had taken his body.
But who? And how? Here's how John remembers it (he refers to himself
as "the other disciple"): "Early Sunday morning, while it was still dark,
Mary Magdalene came to the tomb and found that the stone had been
rolled away from the entrance. She ran and found Simon Peter and the
other disciple, the one whom Jesus loved. She said, 'They have taken
the Lord's body out of the tomb, and I don't know where they have put
him!'" (John 20:1–2).

The tomb had been sealed and carefully guarded. Who could have
taken his body? Who would have? The women stood there poking
around, looking for the body. "They were puzzled, trying to think what
could have happened to it. Suddenly, two men appeared to them, clothed
in dazzling robes. The women were terrified and bowed low before them.

Then the men asked, 'Why are you looking in a tomb for someone who is alive? He isn't here! He has risen from the dead!'" (Luke 24:4–6).

The first Easter morning wasn't a triumphal celebration; it was a swirl of confusion and surprise and terror and amazement and wonder.

The body is gone!

The body is gone?

Each of the Gospel writers tells the story a little differently. Matthew and Mark mention that one angel was there to tell the women that Jesus was alive; Luke points out that there were two. John emphasizes the story of Mary Magdalene; Matthew mentions a group of women arriving. Luke records that Peter ran to the tomb; John remembers running there too and actually beating Peter to the grave.

You get the picture. Each eyewitness remembered different details and emphasized different things, just like real eyewitnesses do. Nothing phony is going on here, nothing suspicious. You can tell the writers didn't get together to try to make sure their facts matched and their stories jibed.

"Okay, guys, one angel or two? What should we say?" says Matthew.

"Two," says Luke. "Definitely two."

Matthew nods. "Right. Let's say two. Everybody got that now?"

John carefully writes the number two down in his notebook.

"Good. Now let's nail down the order here. First there was Mary Magdal—"

"Actually I was with the other women, Matthew. Then I went to get Peter and John and returned to the tomb by myself."

"Um, this is getting a little confusing here. Let's just say first it was the women, then Peter—"

"No, actually I beat him there," says John. "I've always been a pretty good runner—"

"I coulda beat you if I was really trying," says Peter.

"Could not."

"Could too."

"Could not."

"Could too."

"Look," says Matthew. "We'll just lump you two together, okay? Peter and John."

"Why can't it be John and Peter?" says John.

"Oh, brother."

Instead they just tell it like it is. If you look carefully (as many have done) you won't find contradictions (as many had hoped) but only unity and excitement rolled together in coherent confusion.

Try this.

Read for yourself the following accounts of that day: Matthew 28, Mark 16, Luke 24, and John 20. If you'll feel better after piecing the four stories together into one unified narrative, go ahead and have at it. Slice and dice. Personally, I like reading them side by side and letting the flavor of each distinct account impact me. That way I get a better feel for the wild ride they were on that day. It was a roller coaster of questions and joy, of doubt and delight. A new chapter of life was being told in their little corner of the universe.

the chrysalis twitches, quivering.
spring pumps
new life through its veins.
and then,
in a moment of birth, like an
exclamation point coming to life,
it splits open and
the forest bows beneath its wings.
winter has lost. the chrysalis has won.
and the butterfly clings to the branch
as the warm breeze
of promised futures
dries its wings.
      and finally,
      in a moment of complete faith
it lets go and falls into the whirling freedom of the air,
rising on currents of hope that smell like
dew rising to heaven.

easter.

❧

The women had thought Jesus was gone for good. That's obvious because they went to the grave with spices to put on his corpse rather than an omelet to serve him for breakfast. No one expected him to be alive. No one.

They'd wrapped his body in grave clothes and placed him in the ground. Now they were coming back to finish the job. And when they couldn't find the body, nobody said, "Well, of course, he's alive. What'd you expect? He told us a half dozen times he would rise from the dead. Duh."

None of them had caught on yet.

But then the news from an angel: "He is not here; he has risen! Why look for the living among the dead?" (Luke 24:5 NIV). Hope riding on the storm of confusion. And they're all disoriented. Like in a movie when the characters find out that they've been in a dream or a virtual reality world the whole time.

What's real? What's fantasy? If he's not dead and no one stole his body, then he came back to life, and that's not possible . . . is it?

Whiplash.

The last three days had seemed like a nightmare, and now everything seemed like a dream too good to be true. The rules of life and death were being rewritten before their eyes. They looked for him in an empty tomb, but he had already left the boneyard to search for them.

And slowly, the truth began to sink in: Jesus had been dead, but he's not dead any longer. He's alive. Really, truly alive. John, writing in the third person again, tells about his moment of realization in the empty tomb: "Then the other disciple also went in, and he saw and believed—for until then they hadn't realized that the Scriptures said he would rise from the dead" (John 20:8–9).

John got it. He finally understood. He believed.

Dawn had come at last.

✝

touching the unseen

you are the sunlight cutting through
the shadows of my forest,
a breeze carrying the seeds of tomorrow.

you tickle the soft rustlings of spring
poking through the soil of my soul,

you carry my dreams to heaven
on the fairy-like wings of spring.
    all because death couldn't hold
    down a love as great as yours.

alive.

wonder

golgotha cried tears made of nails.
but sunday brings
joy made
of flesh.

✢

As he spoke, he held out his hands for them to see, and he showed
them his feet. Still they stood there doubting, filled with joy and
wonder. Then he asked them, "Do you have anything here to eat?"
They gave him a piece of broiled fish.

—*the memorable reunion of the risen Jesus and his clueless disciples*
(Luke 24:40–42)

I love this part of the story. It's so absurdly human.

Jesus had died. He'd been whipped, beaten, tortured, crucified, and
then buried in a tomb. Now, a couple days later, he appears to his friends
in a locked room and starts trying to convince them he's not dead any
longer.

"Really, guys, I'm alive. Check it out. Look at my hands. See? Does a ghost
have flesh and blood and fingers? Huh? Can a ghost shake your hand?"

And I love how Luke says "he showed them his feet" (24:40). Luke
(who was a doctor, by the way) doesn't say "he showed them the scars
on his feet" but rather, "he showed them his feet."

"I've got feet too, guys! See? How many ghosts have feet? How many
ghosts can do this?" says Jesus as he moonwalks across the room. And

they just stand there in shock until he says, "Hey, you guys got anything to eat around here?"

Someone goes over to the fridge. "Um . . . here's some leftover fish."

"Cool," says Jesus. "I'm famished."

No one could make this stuff up. I mean, if we were in charge of making up a story about a risen Savior, we'd insert a rock concert, or a Billy Graham Crusade, or a victory parade, or at least a press conference. Peter would be the spokesperson. Fox News would carry it.

Instead, the disciples just stand there gawking.

And then there's the whole deal with the broiled fish. If I were making this up, I'd have the disciples hold a banquet and say something reverent like, "Look, O Lord, we have preparedeth for thee a banquet for thine honor and enjoymenteth. For we knewest that thou wouldst riseth againeth from the deadeth just as thou hadst predictedeth. For we hath believedeth in thee!"

Instead it was, "Um, we've got some leftover fish somewhere. Lemme go look for it."

I like that nothing is hidden, nothing is watered down, there's no spin here. This story is so real and earthy and alive with the curious wonder and ridiculous logic of the truth: Jesus is alive, so why shouldn't he have a bite to eat? He must have been hungry. After all, he hadn't eaten since the Last Supper. And being dead can really give you an appetite.

There's nothing to compare this to. People three days dead do not come back to life. We know that. Everything that has a beginning has an end. Everyone knows that.

Except for the Nazarene.

He tips life on its head and turns the end of life into a glorious new beginning. Here's how Paul explained the mystical power of the risen Jesus:

Death swallowed by triumphant Life!
Who got the last word, oh, Death?
Oh, Death, who's afraid of you now?

It was sin that made death so frightening and law-code guilt that gave sin its leverage, its destructive power. But now in a single victorious stroke of Life, all three—sin, guilt, death—are gone, the gift of our Master, Jesus Christ. Thank God!

1 Corinthians 15:54–57 Message

The gifts of the Master are these: freedom, life, hope, new direction, transformation, and intimacy with God. If the cross was the end of the story, we would have no hope. But the cross isn't the end. Jesus didn't escape from death; he conquered it and opened the way to heaven for all who will dare to believe.

The truth of this moment, if we let it sweep over us, is stunning. It means Jesus really is who he claimed to be, we are really as lost as he said we are, and he really is the only way for us to intimately and spiritually connect with God again.

jesus played hide and seek with death.
"3-2-1! ready or not here i come!" she yelled.

but after searching for a while,
she realized jesus had tired of the game and had headed home.
    "come out, come out, wherever you are!"
finally, she just gave up looking
because his home is the one place
she is not allowed to go.

⸎

Frankly, I'm tired of hearing about conferences, seminars, books, and DVDs that will change my life. "This (fill in the blank) will change your life! Attend this life-changing (fill in the blank) and you'll never be the same again! It'll be life changing!"

On the back of one Christian book I recently picked up were three separate quotes by Christian celebrities, all of which promised, "This book will change your life!"

A hernia will change your life. Swallowing two pounds of Ex-Lax will change your life. Getting bitten by a rabid dog will change your life. So will going bankrupt, joining a cult, or getting a tapeworm. All of these things are very life changing.

Change is not always a good thing. What I need isn't change from one thing to another but transformation from who I am into who I was meant to become. Only when God's transforming power touches me can I begin to live the simpler, freer, fresher, more creative, more patient, more passionate, more sacrificial, riskier, rawer, more real, more love-driven life God intended for me to have all along.

That transformation is what awaits all who will dare to enter the story of God. As Paul wrote, "Let God transform you into a new person by changing the way you think" (Romans 12:2).

And that's why the disciples were filled with amazement and terror and wonder on this day. God was begging to transform them. The truth was beginning to sink in. It rocked their world. Everything was backward. Death had lost its stranglehold on life. The hero had won after all. Whiplash after whiplash after whiplash.

Nothing was as it seemed, but actually, everything was getting back to how it was supposed to be all along.

⸙

touching the unseen

questions tremble within me
like paper-thin leaves in the breeze.
but your story is stronger than my pain
and your truth is taking root in my soul.

at last my branches have
touched the edge of blueness,
easing from your caring eyes.

realization.

joy

you are the blossom,
unfold before me.

꙳

The women ran quickly from the tomb. They were very frightened but
also filled with great joy, and they rushed to find the disciples to give
them the angel's message.

*—the reaction of the women who'd come to finish burying Jesus
after they realized he was alive (Matthew 28:8)*

This whole story now has become more like an enfleshed fairy tale than
a history lesson: ancient prophecies coming true, miraculous signs unfolding in a faraway land, magical weddings, demon possessions, mystical meals, an ancient dragon whom the prince has come to vanquish,
midnight betrayals, a king in the guise of a pauper being led away to
face trial, a lover dying for his beloved. And now, a love that death cannot contain.

We all know that in fairy tales and comic books, death is never the
end. Somehow the hero survives to fight another day, or someone finds
the magic potion to awaken the dead. So maybe that's it. Maybe this is
all just a fairy tale or a bedtime story. That's the only possible explanation, right?

Well, normally, yes.

But what if there was a story as true as history yet as fantastic as a fairy tale? A story that was both true in the literal sense and spoke the truth in a metaphysical sense?

The stunning thing about the Easter story is that it claims to be historically accurate and verifiable and yet remains as wonder filled as the greatest fairy tales of all. And if it isn't really true, we shouldn't believe it. In fact, Paul wrote:

> If Christ has not been raised, then your faith is useless, and you are still under condemnation for your sins. In that case, all who have died believing in Christ have perished! And if we have hope in Christ only for this life, we are the most miserable people in the world. But the fact is that Christ has been raised from the dead. He has become the first of a great harvest of those who will be raised to life again.
>
> 1 Corinthians 15:17–20

If this story of Jesus is true, then hope has been reborn and can never die. If it's true, death is not the end of our journey but simply the moment we finally leave shore.

The disciples and the women were beginning to realize this, all of this, all of the implications of Easter morning. So as the dust started to settle and the facts of Jesus's resurrection became established, his friends were filled with unbelievable confusion, hope, wonder, and joy. You can't help but be filled with joy when you finally believe the news of the resurrection:

> The women ran quickly from the tomb. They were very frightened but also **filled with great joy**.
>
> Matthew 28:8

As he spoke, he held out his hands for them to see, and he showed them his feet. Still they stood there doubting, **filled with joy** and wonder.

Luke 24:40–41

He held out his hands for them to see, and he showed them his side. They were **filled with joy** when they saw their Lord!

John 20:20

Any religion that's all somber and serious isn't Christianity. Easter is not an elders' meeting; it's an end zone dance. The curse is over, death is conquered, dawn is here. The words *joy* and *Easter* may not sound the same in English, but they are synonyms in the heart of God.

the sweep of the heavens glistens above me.
sunlight encircles me.
i'm swimming, not in a place, but in a moment,
gathered from eternity and handed to me here.
given to me now.
the mountains sing with words only a soul can hear
faltering against the sky i drink in this air and
tell myself yes, yes, and yes, at last i am
alive.

a new day is awakening in my soul.

✢

Here's the story we've all longed to hear. Ever since Eden, we've known the curse of death and the terrible cost of flirting with the forbidden. We've known death is the end, but it's not any longer. The first harmony has returned and joy, not sorrow, is the final refrain.

Writing to believers facing persecution, Peter encouraged them with this reminder: "You love him even though you have never seen him. Though you do not see him, you trust him; and even now you are happy with a glorious, inexpressible joy" (1 Peter 1:8). Faith leads to joy because, for all true followers of Jesus, death is only paradise in disguise. It's simply the doorway to the party swinging open at last. But for all others, death is the final trip into the tangled forest where the witch lives and all of the bread crumbs have been forever snatched away.

Terror or wonder. Doubt or belief. This moment holds the potential for either—the highway to hell or the gateway to life. Everlasting regret or inexpressible joy.

᠅

touching the unseen

i feel the touch of your hand upon me.
i feel the fire of your presence within me.
i am finally finding out what life and death
    really mean,
as i die to who i was
and you prepare me to be born at last.

i can hear the rhythm of heaven
echoing at last within my soul.

transformation.

scars

a tremor ripples through my soul.
it is either the sound of a stone rolling away
or the deep throaty laughter
of dawn.

❧

He said to Thomas, "Put your finger here and see my hands. Put
   your hand into the wound in my side. Don't be faithless any longer.
   Believe!"

—John, explaining what it took for Thomas to believe
(John 20:27)

I imagine the following conversation (or something like it) happening
in the dawn before my birth.

An angel leans over and says, "See this? This is skin. I'm going to wrap
it tightly around your body. It'll protect you and cover you."

"Skin? But why do I need it?"

"Look at you now, without it! Yuck. Imagine going out into the world
like that!"

"Good point . . ."

"So, anyway, it'll grow with you and then come off when it's supposed
to. But don't take it off too early. That wouldn't be too smart. And
besides, it would hurt."

"Hurt? What is *hurt*?"

"It's something that covers the world like this skin will cover you. Don't be afraid of it, but don't seek it, either. Hurt is the greatest teacher of all, but sometimes the lesson comes too late."

"I don't understand."

"You will."

"Oh . . . well, what's skin like?"

"Natural and comfortable and dry, better than Gore-Tex. And it's sensitive too; it can feel everything from fire to ice, from smooth silk to rough wood. It doesn't like to be out in the sun too long, though, ultraviolet light and all."

"Huh?"

"Never mind. . . . And your skin will want to touch and be touched."

"Touch?"

"Yes, the most wonderful thing skin can do is touch."

"Oh. Anything else?"

"Yes. Skin can also scar."

And then, before she could tell me what scars were, I was born so I could find out for myself.

❧

One time when I was speaking at a church in Kentucky, I mentioned that the disciples recognized Jesus by his scars and that, just like him, we'll have scars in heaven. One rather large woman looked a bit distressed and said, "You mean we won't have perfect bodies in heaven?"

I didn't really know what to say. I guess she assumed she'd look like a supermodel in heaven after spending an entire lifetime eating Twinkies here on earth. I thought about mentioning something about that to her as a helpful little dietary suggestion but decided not to.

Who's to say perfect bodies, heavenly bodies, don't have scars? Jesus had scars when he came back to life. Maybe our scars, our histories of life on this earth, are an essential part of the afterlife. If we can infer anything from the body of the risen Jesus, it seems our scars are the only thing we get to take with us into eternity.

Maybe it's so that when we've been dead for ten billion years and those few moments we had back on earth seem like a dream, we'll be able to say, "Yes, I really did live in that place of skid marks and scars. Yes, he really did come down and die in my place. Yes, I really did believe in him and he really did rise again. Yes, his love really did bring me here."

Or, "Yes, I really did live in that place of skid marks and scars. Yes, he really did come down and die in my place. Yes, I really did scorn him and he really did rise again. Yes, my choices really did send me here."

꙳

Jesus wasn't ashamed of his scars. He didn't apologize for them: "Oh, gee, guys, it's good to see you. Sorry about these scars here. I know they look kinda gross, being fresh and all. But don't worry, they'll heal." No, instead he showed them off like a first grader during show-and-tell. "They're real! Go on, you can touch 'em. It won't hurt!"

Thomas doubted that Jesus was alive. He wanted proof, so Jesus let him feel his scars. And then Thomas believed.

> "My Lord and my God!" Thomas exclaimed.
> Then Jesus told him, "You believe because you have seen me. Blessed are those who haven't seen me and believe anyway."
>
> John 20:28–29

Believe. Believe. Just believe.

Ghosts don't have scars you can touch. They don't eat leftover fish. They don't have feet. But a living Savior does. And a living Savior who walks through walls can walk through even the locked and barred chambers of a human heart.

That's what happens every time someone believes.

Paul believed when a bright light blinded him and a voice from heaven stopped him cold in his tracks. Lydia believed when a few guys showed up at the river and told her about their friend who refused to stay dead. The treasurer of Ethiopia believed when Philip explained an ancient allegory about a lamb. More than three thousand Jews believed when Peter begged them to turn from their sins. God gave them each what they needed in order to believe.

When John saw the empty tomb, he believed. That's what it took for him—an empty tomb. The couple walking on the road to Emmaus believed when the risen Jesus broke some bread and handed it to them. Thomas believed when he touched Jesus's scars. I believed when a bunch of charismatic college students showed me what it looks like to be in love with Jesus.

Jesus will give you the evidence you need. He will do his part. He will whisper into your soul what needs to be said. Your part, the only thing he asks of you, is this: believe. As Jesus said, "This is what God wants you to do: Believe in the one he has sent" (John 6:29).

There, on his skin, is the evidence of how we treat our saviors, of how we act toward God—and how he reacts to us.

Scars and all, God wants to save you. Hopes and dreams and everything; mistakes and wounds and heartaches. All of you. Who you were and who you are. Twinkie-eater or granola-head. Jesus offers to save you body and soul and scars and all.

Believe the story and you'll finally enter it for yourself. Life on this planet is only a preface to the real story God is waiting to tell us in eternity.

⁜

you came back to life with fresh scars and open arms.
you arrive with a constant reminder of our world
pierced and etched upon your skin.
but the deepest scars didn't come from the nails,
and because of that
the healing you offer isn't just skin deep,
  you can heal me all the way down to the bone.
  down to the heart.
i'm ready to enter the tale,
  let your tale enter me.

emergence.

you are a dove hidden in fire.
your flames have grown wings
and flown
through my soul.

☩

I am leaving you with a gift—peace of mind and heart. And the peace I
  give isn't like the peace the world gives.
So don't be troubled or afraid.

  —Jesus of Nazareth, encouraging his friends before he returned to heaven
(John 14:27)

A few years ago I wrote a short drama for the Christmas service at
my church. In the play, a father and his daughter are decorating their
Christmas tree. They goof around for a while, and then the dad says,
"Hand me that angel over there so I can top this bad boy off." (Actually
Jeff Williams, the actor who played the dad in the sketch, came up with
that line. It was so good I had to keep it.) So his daughter, Jessie, reaches
for a decorative angel to put on the top of the tree. Here's how the sketch
plays out from there:

JESSIE: *(looking at the angel)* Dad, can I ask you
        something?

DAD: *(still busy with the tree, distracted)* Sure,
        honey. What's that?

JESSIE:	Didn't the angels say something like, "peace on earth, goodwill toward men?"
DAD:	Yeah, of course they did, Jessie. Peace on earth. That's what Christmas is all about.
JESSIE:	Well, then, why weren't they right?
DAD:	*(after a beat)* What do you mean?
JESSIE:	Why isn't there peace on earth? At school my teacher said we might go to war with Iraq, and then in Israel they're always fighting. And people are still making bombs and blowing up buildings, right?
DAD:	Well, yeah . . .
JESSIE:	So why weren't the angels right, Daddy?
DAD:	Um . . . they were. I mean . . . I always thought they were.
JESSIE:	*(handing him the angel)* I wish they were, don't you, Daddy? Don't you?

(Freeze. Fadeout.)

That's how our Christmas Eve service started. The audience just sat there stunned. It was great. We really freaked people out because we actually brought up the questions they'd wondered about but had been afraid to ask: "Were the angels right or not? If they were, how come there isn't peace on earth? How come there isn't goodwill toward men? If Jesus really is the Prince of Peace, he must have an awfully small kingdom. Is he or isn't he?"

And those are good questions, because our world isn't at peace; I don't know if it's ever been. Peace doesn't live on our planet; it only drops by once in a while for a brief visit on its way through the neighborhood.

So were the angels right or not?

❧

Some people believe that Jesus came to rule in Jerusalem over an earthly kingdom and that when the Jews rejected him, it ruined his plans. I don't agree with that interpretation of his life. Jesus himself said, "I am not an earthly king. If I were, my followers would have fought when I was arrested by the Jewish leaders. But my Kingdom is not of this world" (John 18:36). Taking that into account, along with what he said about his peace being different from the peace this world gives (see John 14:27), I think Jesus came to our planet to invite us to an otherworldly kingdom and offer us an otherworldly peace.

As long as there are greedy, grabby, power-hungry, mean, stupid people on this planet, peace between nations isn't going to happen. And as long as our hearts fight against God, we aren't going to have peace in our lives.

Jesus offers us something different: a fresh relationship with God and the chance to receive true peace in our hearts—a peace that begins now and stretches toward forever.

I didn't used to think I was at war with God. I didn't used to think I was at war with anybody. But when I met Jesus and heard him say, "Follow me," I realized every time I didn't follow him, I was fighting God. Every time I chose to go my way instead of his or to think of myself first instead of others or to flirt with temptation—or basically to act as I had been acting my whole life—I was battling the almighty.

Realizing how deeply rooted your war with God is can shake you up. I'm still reeling from that discovery.

The angels were right. He came to bring peace; it's just that our definition of peace is all messed up.

Our world will always have hatred and prejudice and nuclear weapons and terrorists and suicide bombings. Light and darkness will always clash.

We will never create a heaven on earth. Jesus knew that. On our own we can't even imagine true utopia, let alone initiate it.

Jesus never promised a world without poverty or war or turmoil. In fact, he said we would always have the poor with us and that deception, danger, and conflicts between nations would only escalate as the end of the world draws nearer.

The peace Jesus offers isn't the absence of conflict; it's the adventure of knowing God's presence moment by moment forever. It's a deeper peace than the world can offer—peace with God. True harmony again. Echoes of Eden. The story comes full circle. Easter resonates with the costliest kind of hope and the most intimate kind of peace. A peace Paul says "is far more wonderful than the human mind can understand" (Philippians 4:7).

But it takes humility to admit that your life has been at war with God and that you need to reestablish your relationship with him once again. That's why so few find the narrow way or walk the footpath toward life. Because it's hard to be that honest with God. It hurts. It's humiliating. It's a lot easier to cling to our old lives and self-centered priorities.

That's why his followers are so few.

It's so easy to get tangled up in the nets of everyday living. Yet the irony of life is that a full and cluttered heart is more empty than an empty heart aware of its emptiness. Peace will never come from clutching many things but only from letting go of all but one thing—Jesus.

Because the more we cling to this life, the more we wrap ourselves in its shallow comforts, the more death will bite when she comes to call. But the more we let Jesus untangle us from the baggage of this life, the freer we'll be to become vagabonds of heaven.

the more i die to myself,
the more i
slip from the claws of death
and tumble into the freedom
of life.

paradox.

The soul that's full of ambition and pride is the soul that's full of the emptiness of self. The soul that's drenched in the submission of surrender is the soul that's full of the fullness of God.

Peace will only come into our lives when we realize that the war is over, that we can lay down our arms and stop fighting. After all, God is not the enemy of our hearts.

We are.

God isn't out to get us; he's on our side. He has been ever since the beginning of time when he began dreaming of us. When he fell in love with us.

Jesus declared a truce and signed the peace treaty with his own blood.

Here is the message of Easter: The war is over. Stop battling God. Stop wounding yourself. He's not the enemy. He's the one offering the terms of peace.

⁒

Truth always draws a line in the sand. That's why Jesus told Pontius Pilate, "Everyone on the side of truth listens to me" (John 18:37 NIV). We're not on the side of truth until we're on the side of Jesus. The question each of us must ultimately answer is this: which side will I find myself on when the curtains close, when my boat finally leaves the shore?

Don't look for Jesus in the pages of history; he's dwelling beside you in this present moment. Don't search for him in the cemeteries of religion; he's as close as your next breath and as near as your heartbeat. He offers a peace beyond understanding, a fresh start, a new relationship with God that lasts forever.

Jesus's words to Martha are just as true today as they were twenty-one centuries ago. And his question is just as important: "I am the resurrection and the life. Those who believe in me, even though they die like everyone else, will live again. They are given eternal life for believing in me and will never perish. *Do you believe this*?" (John 11:25–26, emphasis added).

Belief will open the door to the miraculous in your life.

Life has won.

Death has lost.

The curse is over, and the wedding is about to begin.

❧

your spirit is searching for a child of its love.

    make me an ember again.

i feel it descending on the wings of a dove.

    make me an ember again.

the flutter of your feathers,

the touch of your grace,

the chance to finally gaze at your face,

blow over my heart and rekindle the flame.

    make me an ember again.

o spirit! o breath! o right wind of light!

burn off the shame and ignite me—

    ignite!

    make me an ember again!

rebirth.

evermore

our vows are ready.
i can hear you whisper them
to me,
back through time,
awaiting my reply.

✟

The wedding of the Lamb has come, and his bride has made herself
ready.... No longer will there be any curse.... There will be no more
night.... And they will reign for ever and ever ... He who testifies to
these things says, "Yes, I am coming soon." Amen. Come, Lord Jesus.

—John's prophetic visions of the return of Jesus Christ
(Revelation 19:7; 22:3, 5, 20)

Many men had tried to get through. Brave and sturdy men. Soft and
highly cultured men. Some had made it only to the outer edge of the
mesh of thistles and barbs. Some had slashed their way savagely into
the thicket until the thorny limbs—as if with a life of their own—had
curled and entwined. And tightened.

Despite the strength of the man, the screams were always the same.

So each had failed. Each had died. Their bodies remained, though.
Held securely and at odd angles, skewered by the long and narrow thorns.
Embraced by the dark and deadly branches.

The ravens that perch on the high tower had long since picked clean
the remains of those brave princes who'd failed. Anyone who might

wander past the strangely encircled castle would see only glistening bones hanging in the thicket. Patches of white in a sea of tangled black.

And of course, the birds are patient as they wait and watch and wing their way around the tower, their dark, staring eyes searching for more princes. More food.

While inside, beneath their wings, a girl lies. Still and warm.

Waiting.

⸎

The girl is beautiful. Her soft features and delicate cheeks look surreal under the thin layer of dust. It gives her face a vague, ghostly feel. But she is not dead. Her chest moves only slightly to show that she is alive. But her sleep is profound and deeper than deep.

On her thumb is a bead of dried blood. By her bed is a needle-sharp spindle.

Carelessness and curiosity and the allure of the forbidden brought her to this turret with a single staircase and a tapered window overlooking the thicket. She brought it upon herself, and upon all those in the castle. For the curse was real. And now, decades later, the spell still lingers.

Decades upon decades have passed. Time in a bottle. And the thicket has grown and the girl has slept and the stories have whispered their way through the kingdom. Mortal princes have come and died. Those who would rescue her have failed. And so she sleeps.

The curse remains.

The thorns are winning.

⸎

All is still inside the castle. The only movement comes from the sleek dark forms that scurry across the patterned floor. A few rats have found their way beneath the thorns.

The tower rises like a crusty head above the thicket, with a beard of moss and one seeing eye. One window to the world. A single eye that gazes over the thicket, toward a nearby sea, furious and deep and gray. And between the tower and the rocky shore grows a forest with a trail. This is the trail the princes use when they come searching for her. To find her and save her. And love her.

She is only sixteen. Sweet sixteen.

And through every season the sky remains the color of November rain.

⁜

A hundred years, but who's counting? And what's this? The ravens settling onto branches. A rider coming through the forest. Another prince?

Approaching slowly. Confident. But not arrogant like the others. Careful. Thoughtful. Strong.

He dismounts and unsheathes his sword. This man is not just a prince. He is a warrior. He glances at the thicket with a steely eye.

Now the sun is setting, but he is not afraid of the night. With a wild cry he leaps toward the hedge. The birds scatter in fear.

The thorny branches slice at him, writhing like a nest of cornered serpents, piercing his hands and side. Slashing across his head. Aiming for his heart. But he is quick and strong. His swordsmanship is unequaled. And everything in his path splinters and shatters before his blade.

A path begins to form. Crisp moonlight slices wicked shadows all around him, yet he advances through the thorns.

All through the night he fights on. Without a scream. Without a word. Until it is finished. He reaches the tower just as dawn begins to uncurl across the sky. The door is locked, but he has a key fashioned in his father's kingdom. A key that will unlock any door in the castle.

Now through the hall and past the others. Statues frozen in time, not even realizing what they are missing. As if a whole kingdom is holding its breath.

Then he is on the stairs, taking them two at a time. To the upper chamber.

He has waited a lifetime for this moment. He has searched the world for this castle. The stories were true. A girl like no other. A curse whose time was up.

Now he sees her. He is leaning over, his heart racing. Her beauty is unequaled. Just one glance at her face is worth the sting of the thorns. And with his kiss the spell cracks open and the thicket crumbles and the thorns release their grip. The tower is free. Sunlight is alive in the room.

Their eyes meet. Love is born.

"You're more beautiful than I'd ever imagined," he whispers.

She blinks against the light and smiles. The cruel curse is over. He has risked all to rescue her.

"You've set me free," she says, taking his hand.

"Come with me," he offers. And she accepts.

So she will become his bride.

⭢

All those newly awakened are invited to the wedding. And they come. To enjoy the meal and all the festivities. And to welcome this saving prince to their land.

She was a beautiful bride, shedding those old and faded clothes and slipping on the dress her groom had provided for her. They say that her gown was perfect and pure, without a wrinkle, and whiter than the winter hills.

And, ah! The celebration! The feasting! The dancing! Through the day and through the night! They'd had enough sleep to last a thousand lifetimes, and now it was time to celebrate!

And some say that in that distant land, they're still celebrating to this very day.

✢

The adventure isn't over; it's only beginning. Here is my prayer for you as you consider your place in God's story:

I pray that Christ will be more and more at home in your hearts as you trust in him. May your roots go down deep into the soil of God's marvelous love. And may you have the power to understand, as all God's people should, how wide, how long, how high, and how deep his love really is. May you experience the love of Christ, though it is so great you will never fully understand it. Then you will be filled with the fullness of life and power that comes from God.

Ephesians 3:17–19

✢

touching the unseen

tiny wonders of winter dreams
floating softly from the sky
each land with a gentle kiss
on the dark and inky waters
of the cold, unfrozen lake.

there, grace and danger
melt into each other's arms
and become one
as the surface
welcomes the sky into its heart
and the bride is
home at last.

i am falling into your arms.
melt me into yourself
until only you
remain.

union.

notes

harmony

1. I'm indebted to Peter Kreeft's insights about freedom, happiness, and utopia in his book *Making Sense of Suffering* (Ann Arbor, MI: Servant, 1986), which influenced this section. See pages 97–101 in particular.

blood

1. Matthew White, "Deaths by Mass Unpleasantness," Twentieth Century Atlas, March 2004, http://users.erols.com/mwhite28/warstat8.htm.

longing

1. Sadhu Sundar Singh, *Essential Writings*, selected with an introduction by Charles E. Moore (Maryknoll, NY: Orbis, 2000).

silence

1. Alice Gray, Steve Stephens, and John Van Diest, comp., *Lists to Live By* (Sisters, OR: Multnomah, 1999), 90.
2. Coleman Barks, trans., *The Soul of Rumi* (San Francisco: HarperSanFrancisco, 2001), 253.

vagabonds

1. Søren Kierkegaard, *Provocations: Spiritual Writings of Kierkegaard*, ed. Charles E. Moore (Maryknoll, NY: Orbis, 2003), 298.

2. Ibid., 227.

3. Ibid., 88.

skull hill

1. Hans Christian Andersen, *The Complete Hans Christian Andersen Fairy Tales*, ed. Lilly Owens (New York: Avenel Books, 1981), 147–48.

Steven James is an author, storyteller, and poet. He speaks weekly at conferences, churches, and special events across the country, sharing his eclectic blend of drama, comedy, and inspirational storytelling. When he's not traveling or writing, Steven likes going rock climbing, watching science fiction movies, and eating chicken fajitas. He lives with his wife and three daughters in Tennessee.

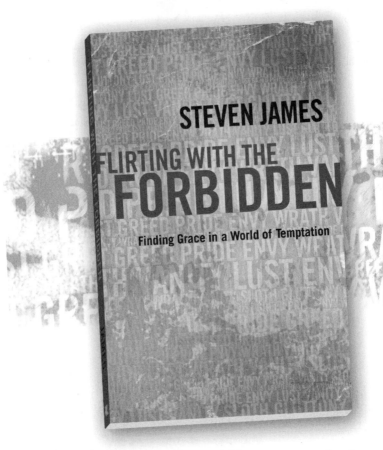